*Stars, flying geese, and nine patch blocks are among the vintage patterns featured in this quilt collection. Stunning appliqués enhance some of the quilts.*

# Contents


Gift Wrapped ........ 2
Kris-Cross ........ 10
Nine Patch Rails ........ 14
Save Your Scraps ........ 18
Desert Stars ........ 24
Trafalgar Square ........ 30
General Instructions ........ 36
Meet Nancy Rink ........ 48




LEISURE ARTS, INC. • Maumelle, Arkansas

# GIFT WRAPPED

## SHOPPING LIST

*Yardage is based on 43"/44" (109 cm/112 cm) wide fabric with a usable width of 40" (102 cm). Fat quarters are approximately 22" x 18" (56 cm x 46 cm.)*

- ☐ 1⁷/₈ yds (1.7 m) of tan texture print fabric for Sweet Sixteen Blocks and Border Blocks A
- ☐ ⁵/₈ yd (57 cm) of green print fabric for Sweet Sixteen Blocks and Border Blocks A
- ☐ 1 fat quarter of light pink stripe fabric for "bows"
- ☐ 1 fat quarter of pink floral print fabric for "bows"
- ☐ 2¹/₂ yds (2.3 m) **total** of 4-5 assorted pink, coral, and dark pink print or plaid fabrics for blocks
- ☐ 3¹/₈ yds (2.9 m) **total** of 5-6 assorted cream print or plaid fabrics for blocks
- ☐ 2¹/₄ yds (2.1 m) **total** of 4-5 assorted brown print fabrics for blocks
- ☐ 3¹/₄ yds (3 m) of brown and cream border stripe for borders
- ☐ 7⁷/₈ yds (7.2 m) of fabric for backing
- ☐ ⁷/₈ yd (80 cm) **total** of assorted fabrics for binding
- ☐ 94" x 118" (239 cm x 300 cm) piece of batting

## CUTTING THE PIECES

*Follow **Rotary Cutting**, page 36, to cut fabric. For yardage, cut all strips from the selvage-to-selvage width of the fabric unless otherwise stated. For fat quarters, cut strips parallel to the long edge. Borders are cut longer than needed and will be trimmed to fit quilt top center. All measurements include ¹/₄" seam allowances.*

***Note:** On fabric combinations for the Wrapped Boxes blocks, each block needs a matching set of 8 **squares A** and 4 **squares F** for the "box" and a matching set of 8 **squares A** and 8 **rectangles B** for the "ribbon" and outer corners. Four matching **rectangles B** make the star "bow" in the middle of the block. The block background consists of 8 matching **squares A** and 8 matching **rectangles B**.*

### From tan texture fabric:

- Cut 4 strips 2" wide. From these strips, cut 68 **squares A** 2" x 2".
- Cut 8 strips 2" wide. From these strips, cut 78 **rectangles B** 2" x 3¹/₂".
- Cut 2 strips 2" wide. From these strips, cut 10 **rectangles C** 2" x 6¹/₂".
- Cut 3 strips 2" wide. From these strips, cut 10 **rectangles D** 2" x 9¹/₂".
- Cut 9 strips 2" wide. From these strips, cut 68 **rectangles E** 2" x 5".
- Cut 1 strip 6¹/₂" wide. From this strip, cut 4 **squares G** 6¹/₂" x 6¹/₂".

### From green print fabric:

- Cut 10 strips 2" wide. From these strips, cut 192 **squares A** 2" x 2".

**Finished Quilt Size:** 86" x 110" (218 cm x 279 cm)

**Finished Wrapped Boxes Block Size:** 12" x 12" (30 cm x 30 cm)

**Finished Sweet Sixteen Block Size:** 12" x 12" (30 cm x 30 cm)

**Finished Border Block A Size:** 6" x 12" (15 cm x 30 cm)

**Finished Border Block B Size:** 6" x 12" (15 cm x 30 cm)

### From light pink stripe fat quarter:

- Cut 8 strips 2" x 21". From these strips, cut 48 **rectangles B** 2" x 3½".

### From pink floral print fat quarter:

- Cut 4 strips 2" x 21". From these strips, cut 24 **rectangles B** 2" x 3½".

### From assorted pink, coral, and dark pink print or plaid fabrics:

- Cut a **total** of 144 **squares A** 2" x 2".
- Cut a **total** of 104 **rectangles B** 2" x 3½".
- Cut a **total** of 24 **rectangles C** 2" x 6½".
- Cut a **total** of 24 **rectangles D** 2" x 9½".
- Cut a **total** of 32 **squares F** 3½" x 3½".

### From assorted cream print or plaid fabrics:

- Cut a **total** of 224 **squares A** 2" x 2".
- Cut a **total** of 192 **rectangles B** 2" x 3½".
- Cut a **total** of 48 **rectangles C** 2" x 6½".
- Cut a **total** of 48 **rectangles D** 2" x 9½".

### From assorted brown print fabrics:

- Cut a **total** of 336 **squares A** 2" x 2".
- Cut a **total** of 64 **rectangles B** 2" x 3½".
- Cut a **total** of 40 **squares F** 3½" x 3½".

### From brown and cream border stripe fabric:

- Cut 2 *lengthwise* **side borders** 7" x 112", centered on a cream stripe.
- Cut 2 *lengthwise* **top/bottom borders** 7" x 88", centered on a cream stripe.

### From binding fabrics:

- Cut assorted **binding strips** 2¼" wide in various lengths to total 12 yds when sewn together diagonally end to end.

## MAKING THE WRAPPED BOXES BLOCKS

*Follow* ***Machine Piecing****, page 37, and* ***Pressing****, page 39, to make quilt top. Use ¼" seam allowances throughout.*

1. Matching right sides, place a "box" **square A** on one end of a "bow" **rectangle B**. Draw a diagonal line on **square A**. Sew along the drawn line ***(Fig. 1)***. Trim the seam allowances to ¼" ***(Fig. 2)***. Press open to make **Unit 1**. Make a **total** of 4 matching Unit 1's.

**Fig. 1**

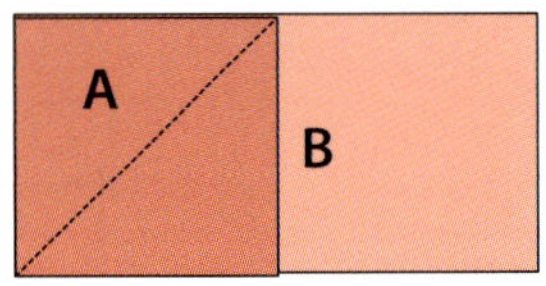


**Fig. 2**

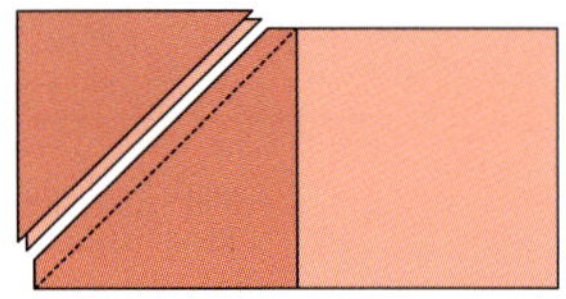

**Unit 1**
(make a **total** of 4 matching Unit 1's)

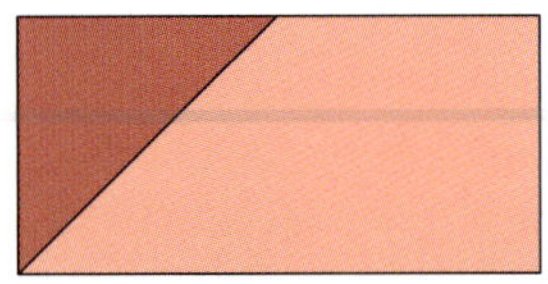

2. Repeat Step 1, placing a "ribbon" **square A** on opposite end of **Unit 1** to make **Unit 2**. Make a **total** of 4 matching Unit 2's.

**Unit 2**
(make a **total** of 4 matching Unit 2's)

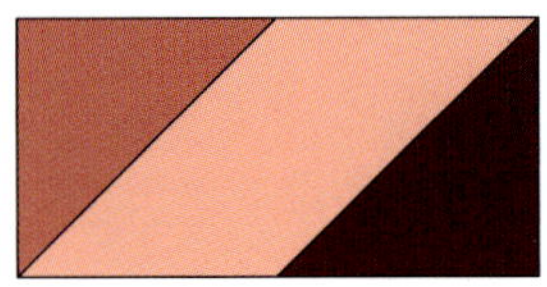

3. Sew 1 "box" **square A**, 1 Unit 2, 1 "box" **square F**, and 1 "ribbon" **rectangle B** together to make **Unit 3**. Make a **total** of 4 matching Unit 3's.

**Unit 3**

(make a **total** of 4 matching Unit 3's)

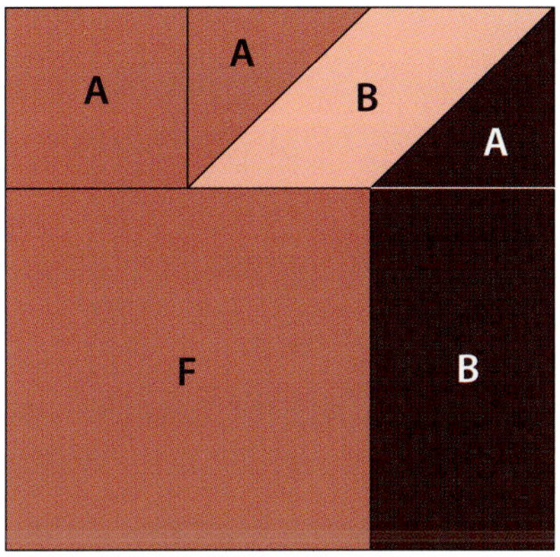


4. Paying attention to the orientation, sew 4 Unit 3's together to make **Unit 4**.

**Unit 4**

5. Paying attention to the orientation, repeat Step 1, placing a cream "background" **square A** on one end of a "ribbon" **rectangle B** and another cream "background" **square A** on the opposite end of **rectangle B** to make **Unit 5.** Make a total of 4 matching Unit 5's.

**Unit 5**

(make a **total** of 4 matching Unit 5's)

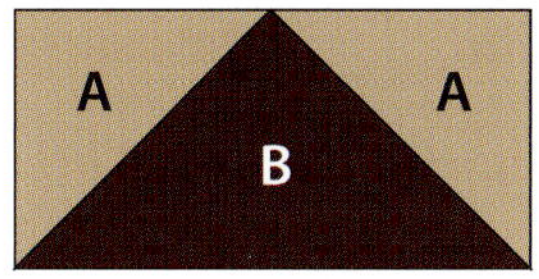


6. Sew 1 **Unit 5** and 2 cream "background" **rectangles B** together to make **Unit 6**. Make a total of 4 matching Unit 6's.

**Unit 6**

(make a **total** of 4 matching Unit 6's)

7. Sew 1 Unit 6 to opposite sides of Unit 4.
8. Sew 1 "ribbon" **square A** to each end of each remaining Unit 6 to make **Unit 7**. Make a total of 2 matching Unit 7's.

**Unit 7**

(make a **total** of 2 matching Unit 7's)

9. Sew 1 Unit 7 to remaining sides of Unit 4 to make a **Wrapped Boxes Block** (Colorway 1). Make a **total** of 12 Wrapped Boxes Blocks with cream backgrounds (Colorway 1).
10. Repeat Steps 1 - 9 to make a **total** of 6 Wrapped Boxes Blocks with cream ribbon and pink backgrounds (Colorway 2).

**Wrapped Boxes Block**
Colorway 1
(make 12)

**Wrapped Boxes Block**
Colorway 2
(make 6)

## MAKING THE SWEET SIXTEEN BLOCKS

1. Sew 2 assorted brown **squares A** and 2 green **squares A** together to make a **4-Patch Unit A**. Make 17 4-Patch Unit A's.

**4-Patch Unit A**
(make 17)

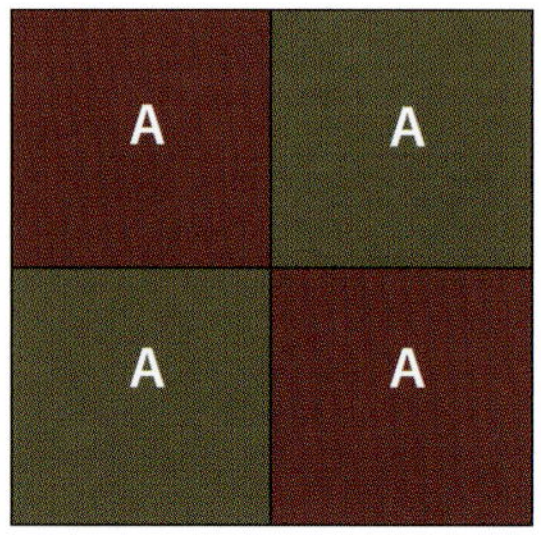


2. Sew 1 pink **rectangle B** to opposite sides of the 4-Patch Unit A. Sew a green **square A** and a brown **square A** to opposite ends of a cream **rectangle B** to make **Unit 8**. Make 34 Unit 8's. Paying attention to the orientation of green and brown squares, sew 1 Unit 8 to each remaining side of the 4-Patch Unit A.

**Unit 8**
(make 34)

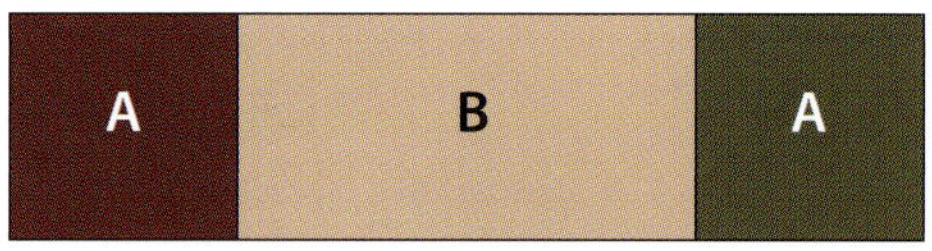


3. Continue adding pink and cream **rectangles C** and **rectangles D** and brown and green **squares A** in the same manner to make a **Sweet Sixteen Block**. Make a total of 7 Sweet Sixteen Blocks in Colorway 1.

4. Repeat in the same manner using pink, tan, and cream rectangles B, C, and D to make 10 **Sweet Sixteen Blocks** in Colorway 2.

**Sweet Sixteen Block**
Colorway 1
(make 7)

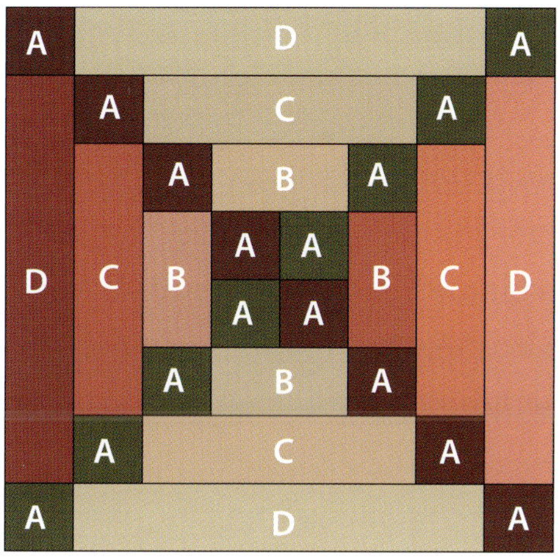


**Sweet Sixteen Block**
Colorway 2
(make 10)

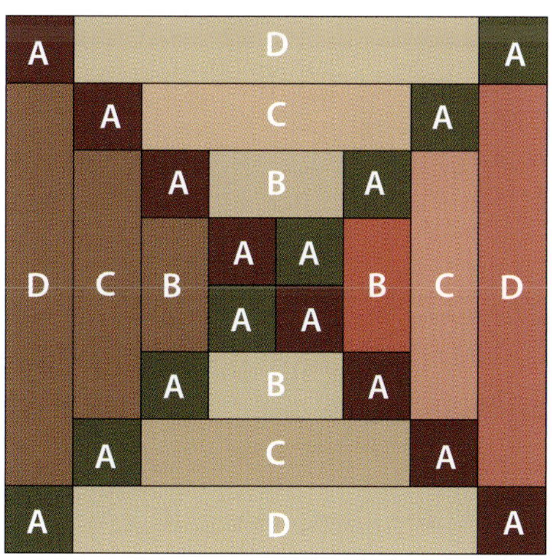


## MAKING BORDER BLOCK A

1. Sew 1 brown **square A**, 1 green **square A**, and 2 tan **squares A** together to make **Unit 9**. Make 14 Unit 9's. Press seam allowances toward brown and green squares.

**Unit 9**
(make 14)

2. Sew 1 brown **square A** and 1 green **square A** to each end of 1 cream **rectangle B** to make **Unit 10**. Make 14 Unit 10's. Press seam allowances toward squares.

**Unit 10**
(make 14)

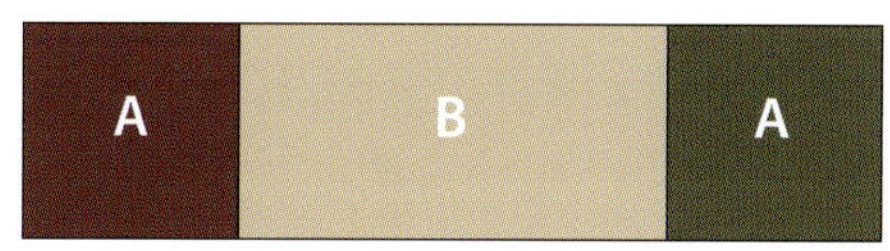


3. Sew Unit 9 and Unit 10 together. Sew 1 tan **rectangle B** to each end to make **Unit 11**. Make 14 Unit 11's.

**Unit 11**
(make 14)

4. Referring to diagram for color placement, continue adding **squares A, rectangles C**, **rectangles D**, and **rectangles E** in the same manner to make a **Border Block A**. Make a total of 14 Border Block A's.

**Border Block A**

(make 14)

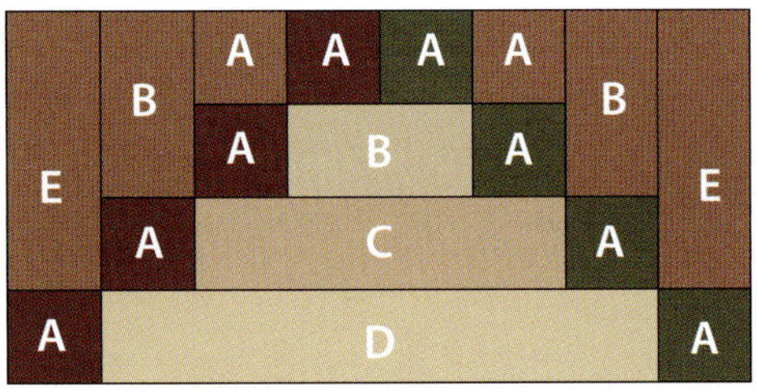


## MAKING BORDER BLOCK B

1. Sew 2 cream **squares A** and 2 tan **squares A** together to make a **4-Patch Unit B**. Add a tan **rectangle B** to the right side of the 4-Patch Unit B. Press the seam allowances toward rectangle **B**. Sew 1 tan **rectangle B** and 1 cream **square A** together. Press seam allowances toward rectangle **B**. Sew Units together to make **Unit 12**.

**4-Patch Unit B**

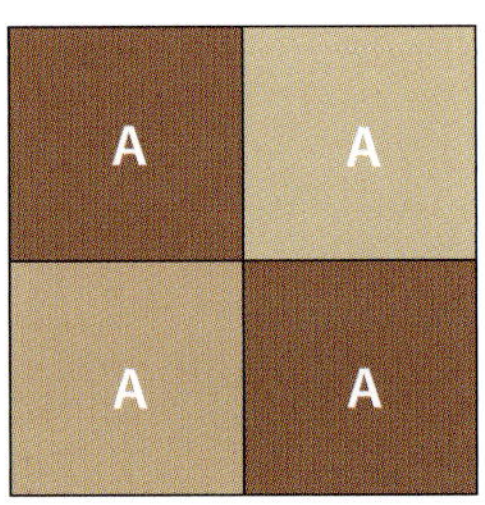


**Unit 12**

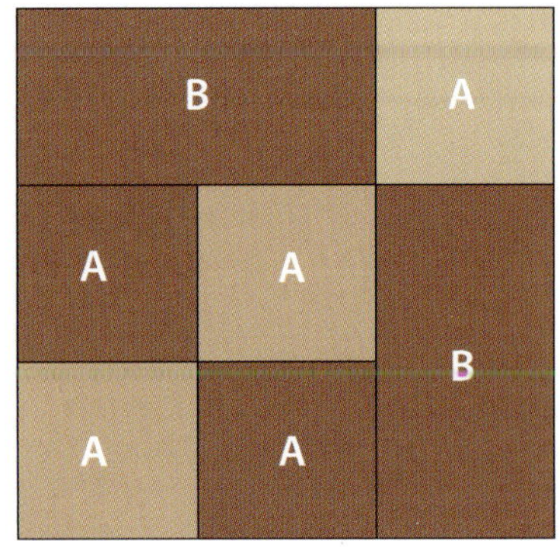


2. Sew 1 tan **rectangle E** to right side of the Unit 12. Press seam allowances toward rectangle **E**. Sew 1 tan **rectangle E** and 1 cream **square A** together. Press seam allowances toward rectangle **E**. Sew this to top of Unit 12 to make **Unit 13**.

**Unit 13**

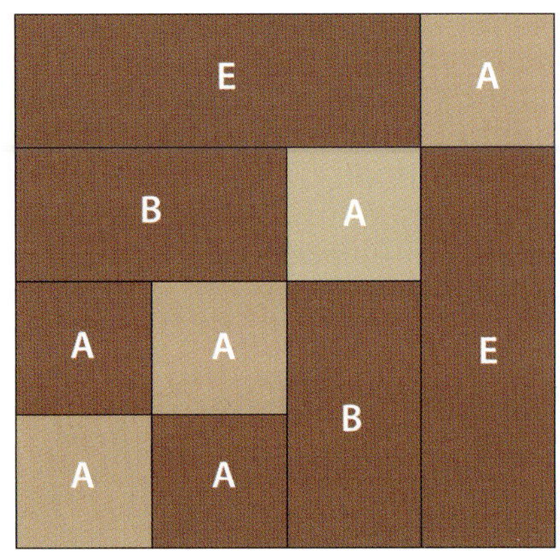


3. Repeat Steps 1-2 to make 20 Unit 13's.
4. Join 2 Unit 13's together to make **Border Block B**. Make 10 Border Block B's.

**Border Block B**

(make 10)

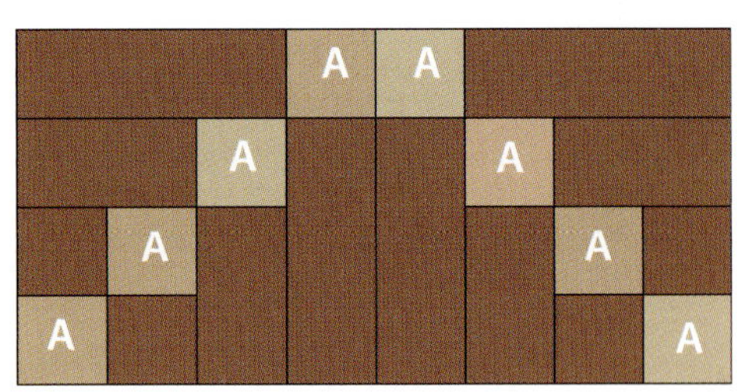

## ASSEMBLING THE QUILT TOP

*Refer to **Quilt Top Diagram** to assemble quilt top. Note that the Sweet Sixteen Colorway 1 Blocks are positioned so that the cream rectangles touch the cream rectangles of the Wrapped Boxes Colorway 1 Blocks and the pink rectangles of the Wrapped Boxes Colorway 2 Blocks.*

1. Arrange the Wrapped Boxes Blocks, Sweet Sixteen Blocks, Border Block A's, Border Block B's, and tan **square G's**.
2. Sew the Blocks and square G's together in horizontal rows. Sew the rows together.
3. Refer to **Adding Mitered Borders**, page 39, to sew **side borders** and **top/bottom borders** to quilt top.

## COMPLETING THE QUILT

1. Follow **Quilting**, page 42, to mark, layer, and quilt as desired. Quilt shown is quilted with a feather design around each block and a vine in the outer border.
2. Follow **Making a Hanging Sleeve**, page 44, if a hanging sleeve is desired.
3. Sew **binding strips** together end to end diagonally. Follow **Attaching Binding with Mitered Corners**, page 45, to bind quilt.

**Quilt Top Diagram**

# KRIS-CROSS

*To create the scrappy look of this quilt, mix and match the various fabrics in each block. The cutting instructions provide you with a few extra squares and strips to allow you the freedom to play with block design. To increase the scrappy look, add a few additional fat eighths or scraps from your stash.*

## SHOPPING LIST

*Yardage is based on 43"/44" (109 cm/112 cm) wide fabric with a usable width of 40" (102 cm). A fat quarter measures approximately 22" x 18" (56 cm x 46 cm.)*

- ☐ 15-16 fat quarters or approximately 4 yds (3.7 m) **total** of coordinating print fabrics for blocks
- ☐ 7/8 yd (80 cm) of red print fabric for inner border and bindings
- ☐ 2 yds (1.8 m) of floral print fabric for outer border
- ☐ 4 1/2 yds (4.1 m) of fabric for backing
- ☐ 70" x 79" (178 cm x 201 cm) piece of batting

## CUTTING THE PIECES

*Follow* ***Rotary Cutting****, page 36, to cut fabric. For yardage, cut all strips from the selvage-to-selvage width of the fabric unless otherwise stated. For fat quarters, cut strips parallel to the short edge. Outer borders are cut longer than needed and will be trimmed to fit quilt top center. All measurements include 1/4" seam allowances.*

### From *each* fat quarter:

- Cut 6 **short strips** 1 1/2" x 18".
- Cut 2 strips 3 1/2" x 18". From these strips, cut 10 **squares** 3 1/2" x 3 1/2".

### From red print fabric:

- Cut 6 **inner border strips** 1 1/2" wide.
- Cut 8 **binding strips** 2 1/4" wide.

### From floral print fabric:

- Cut 2 *lengthwise* **outer side borders** 7 1/2" x 60 1/2".
- Cut 2 *lengthwise* **outer top/bottom borders** 7 1/2" x 65 1/2".

**Finished Quilt Size:** 62" x 71" (157 cm x 180 cm)
**Finished Block Size:** 9" x 9" (23 cm x 23 cm)

## MAKING THE BLOCKS

*Follow **Machine Piecing**, page 37, and **Pressing**, page 39, to make quilt top. Use ¼" seam allowances throughout.*

1. Sew together 2 matching **short strips** and one contrasting **short strip**. Press the seam allowances toward the center strip. Cut the pieced strip into four 3½" segments *(**Fig. 1**)*.

**Fig. 1**

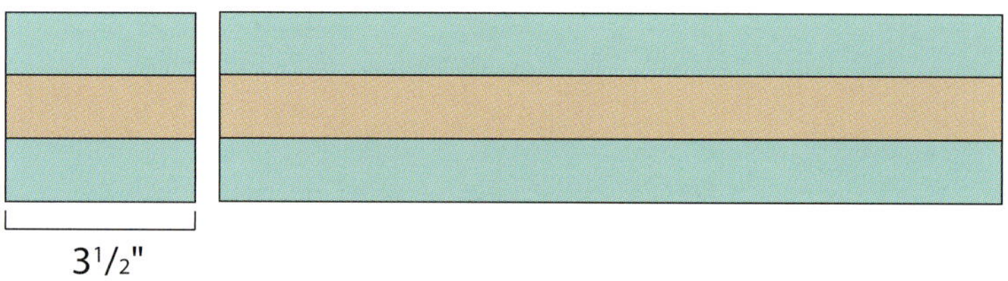


2. Arrange 4 matching **squares**, 1 contrasting **square**, and 4 pieced segments. Sew the pieces together in rows, pressing the seam allowances away from the pieced segments. Sew the rows together. Repeat to make a **total** of 30 Blocks.

**Block** (make 30)

## ASSEMBLING THE QUILT TOP

*Refer to **Quilt Top** to assemble quilt top.*

1. Sew 5 Blocks together to make a Row. Make 6 Rows. Sew the Rows together.
2. Using diagonal seams, sew **inner border strips** together to make one continuous strip *(**Fig. 2**)*.

**Fig. 2**

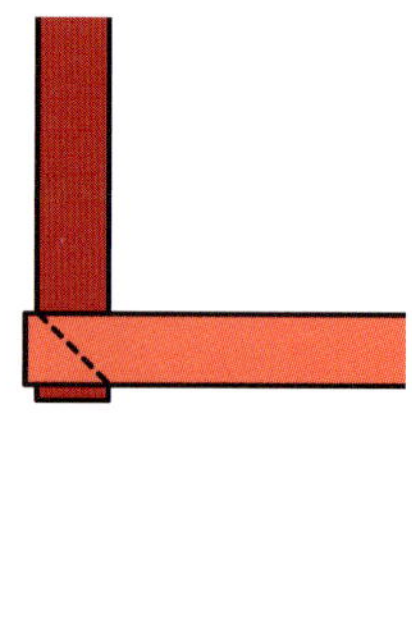

3. Measure *length* across center of quilt top center. Cut 2 **inner side borders** from continuous strip. Matching centers and corners, sew inner side borders to quilt top center.
4. Measure *width* across center of quilt top center (including added borders). Cut 2 **inner top/bottom borders** from continuous strip. Matching centers and corners, sew inner top/bottom borders to quilt top center.
5. Repeat Steps 3-4 to add **outer side**, then **outer top/bottom borders**.

**Quilt Top**

## COMPLETING THE QUILT

1. Follow **Quilting**, page 42, to mark, layer, and quilt as desired. Quilt shown is quilted with an all-over leaf design in the quilt top center, in the ditch along each border, and a feather design in the outer border.
2. Follow **Making a Hanging Sleeve**, page 44, if a hanging sleeve is desired.
3. Sew **binding strips** together end to end diagonally. Follow **Attaching Binding with Mitered Corners**, page 45, to bind quilt.

# NINE PATCH RAILS

*In Nancy's quilt, the Nine-Patch Blocks are scrappy. Some of the pieces in each block match, others don't. Feel free to mix and match your scraps as Nancy did.*

## SHOPPING LIST

*Yardage is based on 43"/44" (109 cm/112 cm) wide fabric with a usable width of 40" (102 cm).*

- ☐ 3 1/2 - 3 3/4 yds (3.2 m - 3.4 m) **total** of assorted light print fabrics
- ☐ 2 3/4 - 3 yds (2.5 m - 2.7 m) **total** of assorted medium and dark print fabrics
- ☐ 7/8 yd (80 cm) of red tone-on-tone fabric for setting triangles
- ☐ 5/8 yd (57 cm) of beige print fabric for inner border
- ☐ 2 3/4 yds (2.5 m) of red print fabric for outer border
- ☐ 7/8 yd (80 cm) of fabric for binding
- ☐ 8 1/2 yds (7.8 m) of fabric for backing
- ☐ 100" x 100" (254 cm x 254 cm) piece of batting

## CUTTING THE PIECES

*Follow* ***Rotary Cutting****, page 36, to cut fabric. Cut all strips from the selvage-to-selvage width of the fabric unless otherwise stated. Outer borders are cut longer than needed and will be trimmed to fit quilt top center. All measurements include 1/4" seam allowances.*

### From assorted light print fabrics:

- Cut 288 **rectangles A** 2" x 5".
- Cut 484 **squares B** 2" x 2".

### From assorted medium and dark print fabrics:

- Cut 144 **rectangles A** 2" x 5".
- Cut 605 **squares B** 2" x 2".

### From red tone-on-tone fabric:

- Cut 3 strips 7 3/4" wide. From these strips, cut 11 squares 7 3/4" x 7 3/4". Cut each square **twice** diagonally to make 44 **triangles C**.*
- Cut 1 strip 4 1/2" wide. From this strip, cut 2 squares 4 1/2" x 4 1/2". Cut each square **once** diagonally to make 4 **triangles D**.*

### From beige print fabric:

- Cut 9 **inner border strips** 2" wide.

### From red print fabric:

- Cut 2 *lengthwise* **outer side borders** 6 1/2" x 83 1/2".
- Cut 2 *lengthwise* **outer top/bottom borders** 6 1/2" x 95 1/2".

### From binding fabric:

- Cut 11 **binding strips** 2 1/4" wide.

*These pieces are cut slightly oversized to allow for trimming after construction.

**Finished Quilt Size:** 92" x 92" (234 cm x 234 cm)

**Finished Block Size:** $4^1/_2$" x $4^1/_2$" (11 cm x 11 cm)

*Quilted by Eve Hall.*

## MAKING THE RAIL BLOCKS

*Follow **Machine Piecing**, page 37, and **Pressing**, page 39, to make quilt top. Use $^1/_4$" seam allowances throughout.*

1. Sew together two light print **rectangles A** and one medium or dark print **rectangle A** to make a **Rail Block**. Press the seam allowances toward the medium or dark print fabric. Make 144 Rail Blocks.

**Rail Block** (make 144)

## MAKING THE NINE PATCH BLOCKS

1. Sew together four light print **squares B** and five medium or dark print **squares B** to make a **Nine Patch Block**. Sew the squares together in rows, pressing the seam allowances toward the darker fabric. Sew the rows together. Make 121 Nine Patch Blocks.

**Nine Patch Block** (make 121)

## ASSEMBLING THE QUILT TOP

*Refer to **Quilt Top** to assemble quilt top.*

1. Alternating the Blocks, sew the Blocks and **triangle C's** together in diagonal rows. Sew the rows together.
2. Sew a **triangle D** to each corner.
3. Trim the quilt top to measure 76$^1/_2$" x 76$^1/_2$".
4. Using diagonal seams, sew **inner border strips** together to make one continuous strip ***(Fig. 1)***.

**Fig. 1**

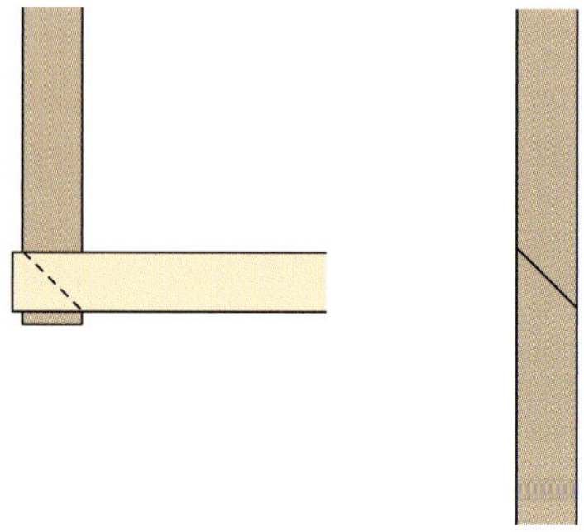

5. Measure *length* across center of quilt top center. Cut 2 **inner side borders** from continuous strip. Matching centers and corners, sew inner side borders to quilt top center.
6. Measure *width* across center of quilt top center (including added borders). Cut 2 **inner top/bottom borders** from continuous strip. Matching centers and corners, sew inner top/bottom borders to quilt top center.
7. Repeat Steps 5-6 to add **outer top/bottom**, then **outer side borders**.

**Quilt Top**

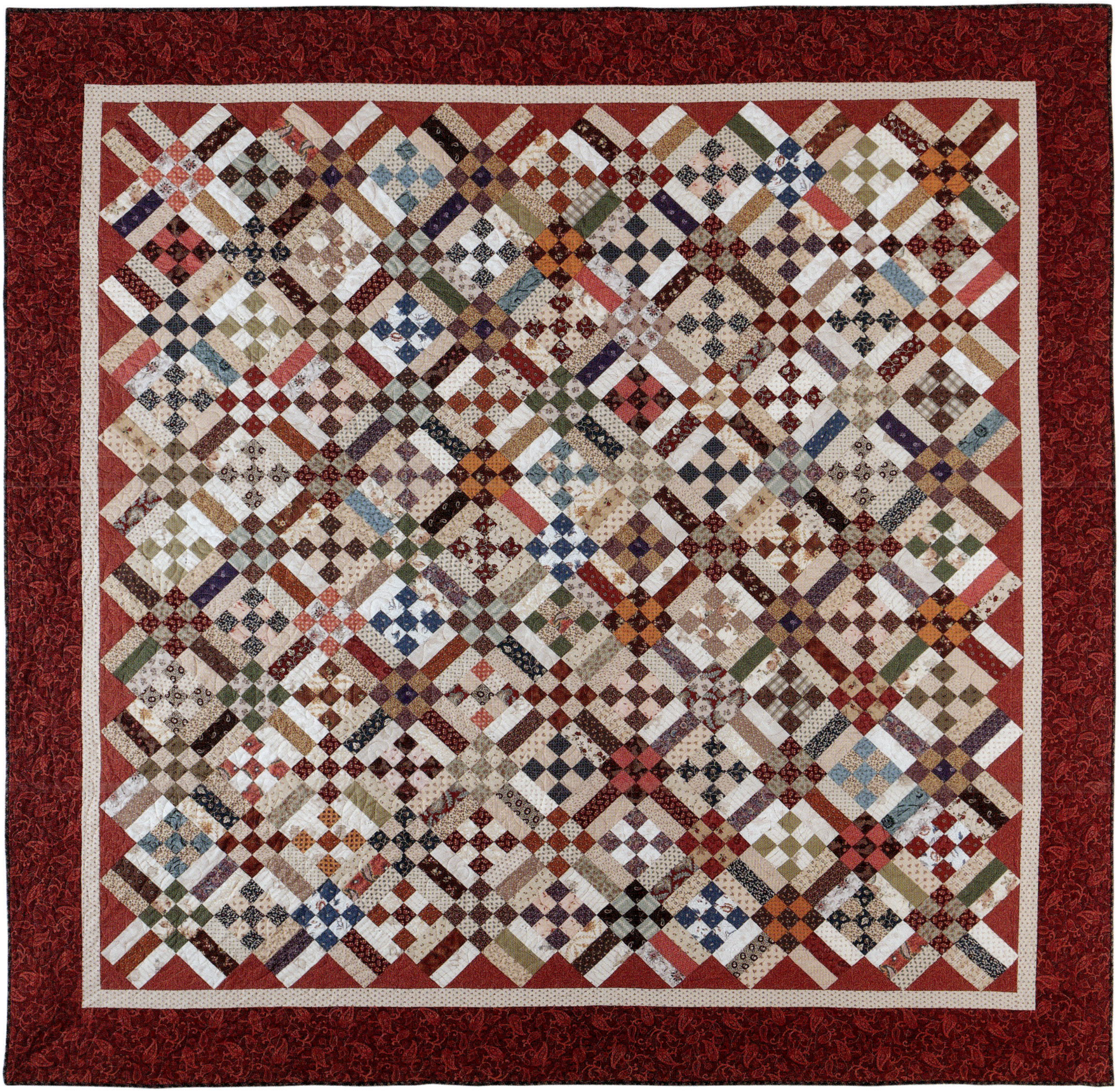

## COMPLETING THE QUILT

1. Follow **Quilting**, page 42, to mark, layer, and quilt as desired. Quilt shown is quilted with all-over meandering design.
2. Follow **Making a Hanging Sleeve**, page 44, if a hanging sleeve is desired.
3. Sew **binding strips** together end to end diagonally. Follow **Attaching Binding with Mitered Corners**, page 45, to bind quilt.

# SAVE YOUR SCRAPS

## SHOPPING LIST

*Yardage is based on 43"/44" (109 cm/112 cm) wide fabric with a usable width of 40" (102 cm). A fat quarter measures approximately 22" x 18" (56 cm x 46 cm).*

- ☐ 1 1/2 - 2 yds (1.4 m - 1.8 m) **total** of assorted light print fabrics for Double Nine Patch and Shoo Fly Blocks
- ☐ 2 - 2 1/4 yds (1.8 m - 2.1 m) **total** of assorted medium and dark print fabrics for blocks and binding
- ☐ 3/8 yd (34 cm) **total** of assorted blue print fabrics for Shoo Fly Blocks
- ☐ 5/8 yd (57 cm) **total** of assorted rust print fabrics for inner border and Prairie Dresden Block centers
- ☐ 1 yd (91 cm) of light tone-on-tone print fabric for Prairie Dresden Block backgrounds
- ☐ 1 7/8 yds (1.7 m) of blue print fabric for outer border
- ☐ 4 yds (3.7 m) of fabric for backing
- ☐ 72" x 72" (183 cm x 183 cm) piece of batting
- ☐ EZ Quilting® Easy Dresden Quilt Ruler
- ☐ Pieces Be With You® Prairie Pointer Pressing Tool
- ☐ freezer paper
- ☐ liquid starch
- ☐ small paintbrush
- ☐ chopstick or awl
- ☐ fabric glue (optional)

## CUTTING THE PIECES

*Follow* ***Rotary Cutting****, page 36, to cut fabric. For yardage, cut all strips from the selvage-to-selvage width of the fabric unless otherwise stated. For fat quarters, cut strips parallel to the long edge. Outer border strips are cut longer than needed and will be trimmed to fit quilt top center. All measurements include 1/4" seam allowances.*

### From assorted light print fabrics:

- Cut 240 **squares A** 1 1/2" x 1 1/2".
- Cut 80 **squares B** 3 1/2" x 3 1/2".

### From assorted medium and dark print fabrics:

- Cut 2 1/2" wide **strips** to total approximately 280" of length for the Dresden Wedges.
- Cut 300 **squares A** 1 1/2" x 1 1/2".
- Cut assorted **binding strips** 2 1/4" wide in various lengths to total 8 yds when sewn together diagonally end to end.

### From assorted blue print fabrics:

- Cut 16 **squares A** 1 1/2" x 1 1/2".
- Cut 4 **squares B** 3 1/2" x 3 1/2".

### From assorted rust print fabrics:

- Cut assorted **inner border strips** 2 1/2" wide in random lengths to total approximately 220" when sewn together diagonally end to end.

### From light tone-on-tone print fabric:

- Cut 9 **background squares** 10" x 10".

### From blue print fabric:

- Cut 2 *lengthwise* **outer side borders** 7 1/2" x 49 1/2".
- Cut 2 *lengthwise* **outer top/bottom borders** 7 1/2" x 67 1/2".

**Finished Quilt Size:** 64" x 64" (163 cm x 163 cm)
**Finished Block Size:** 9" x 9" (23 cm x 23 cm)

## MAKING THE PRAIRIE DRESDEN BLOCKS

*Follow **Machine Piecing**, page 37, and **Pressing**, page 39, to make quilt top. Use 1/4" seam allowances throughout.*

1. For the Dresden Wedges, align the 2 1/2" line on the Easy Dresden Ruler with the top edge of a **strip**. Cut along each side of the ruler to cut a wedge. Rotate the ruler and align the 2 1/2" line on the ruler with the bottom edge of the strip; cut. Repeat this process ***(Fig. 1)*** until you have cut a total of 180 wedges.

**Fig. 1**

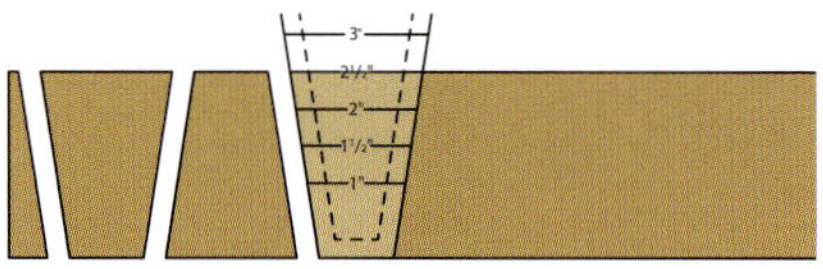

2. For each wedge, fold the wide end, right sides together, and stitch using a short stitch length ***(Fig. 2)***. Trim the point from the folded edge at an angle ***(Fig. 3)***. Using the Prairie Pointer Pressing Tool, align the seam with the center line on the tool; press the seam open ***(Fig. 4)***. Turn wedge right side out; insert pressing tool and press ***(Fig. 5)***.

**Fig. 2**

**Fig. 3**

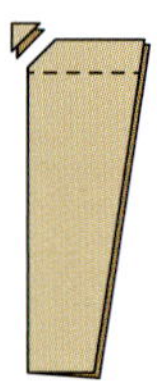

**Fig. 4**

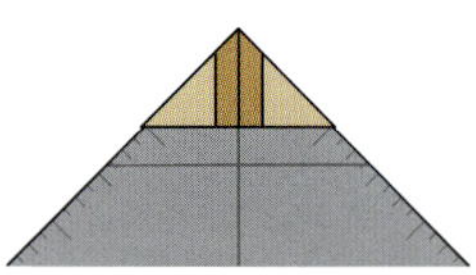

**Fig. 5**

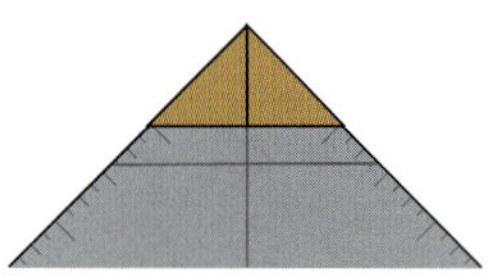

3. Matching right sides and aligned the pointed ends, place 2 wedges together. Backstitching at beginning and end and beginning stitching at the folded edge, sew the wedges together along one edge ***(Fig. 6)***; press open. Join five wedges in this manner. Press seam allowances open. Make a total of 36 **Wedge Units**.

**Fig. 6**

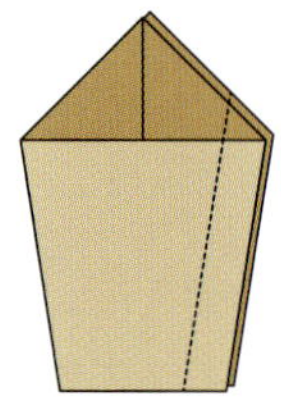

**Wedge Unit** (make 36)

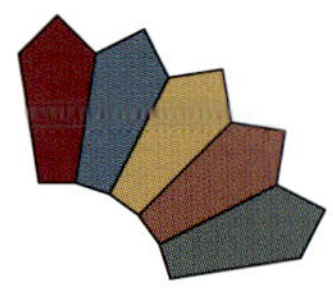

4. Sew 4 Wedge Units together to make a **Dresden Flower**. Make a total of 9 Dresden Flowers.

**Dresden Flower** (make 9)

5. Press each **background square** horizontally and vertically through the center to create registration marks.
6. Aligning the points of the wedges with the registration marks, position a Dresden Flower on a background square; pin or glue the flower in place with small dabs of glue.
7. Trace the circle template 9 times onto freezer paper. Keeping both pieces dull side up, press the traced freezer paper to an unmarked sheet of freezer paper. Cut out the two-layered freezer paper templates.
8. Position one template on the wrong side of the rust print fabric. Iron the template to the fabric, shiny side down. Trim fabric, leaving an approximately $^{3}/_{8}$" seam allowance.
9. Use the paintbrush to brush starch on the seam allowance. Incrementally turn the seam allowance over the edge of the freezer paper circle using a chopstick or awl, adding starch and pressing the seam allowance in place as you go. Remove the freezer paper.

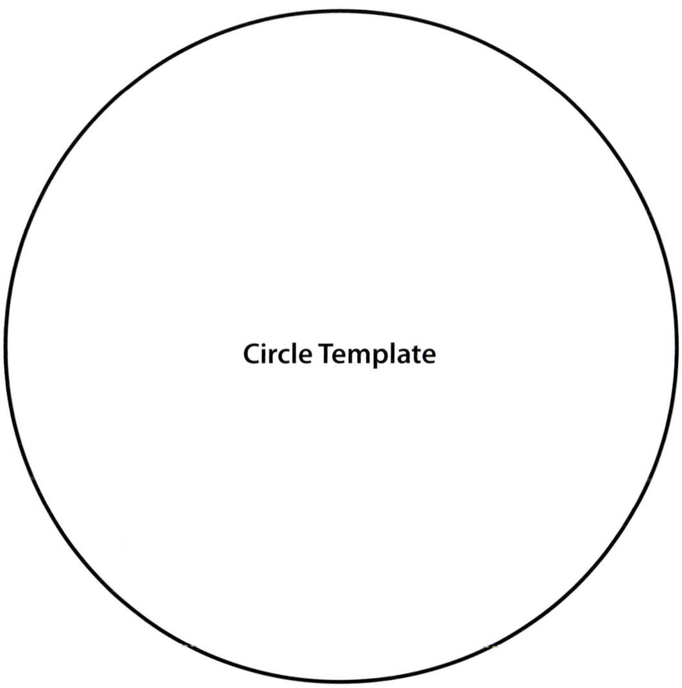


10. Position the circle on the flower. Pin or glue the circle in place with small dabs of glue. Refer to **Blind Stitch**, page 47, to sew the circle in place.
11. Press the block from the wrong side. Centering the flower, trim the block to $9^{1}/_{2}$" x $9^{1}/_{2}$" to make the **Prairie Dresden Block**. Make a total of 9 Prairie Dresden Blocks.

**Prairie Dresden Block**

## MAKING THE DOUBLE NINE PATCH BLOCKS

1. Sew together four light print **squares A** and five medium or dark print squares A to make a **Nine Patch Block**. Sew the squares together in rows, pressing the seam allowances toward the darker fabric. Sew the rows together. Make 60 Nine Patch Blocks.

**Nine Patch Block** (make 60)

2. Sew together four light print **squares B** and five Nine Patch Blocks to make a **Double Nine Patch Block**. Sew the units together in rows, pressing the seam allowances toward the squares B. Sew the rows together. Make 12 Double Nine Patch Blocks.

**Double Nine Patch Block** (make 12)

## MAKING THE SHOO FLY BLOCKS

1. Draw a diagonal line from corner to corner on the wrong side of the blue print **squares A**. Matching right sides, place one blue print square A on one light print **square B**. Stitch on the drawn line; trim the seam allowances to 1/4" ***(Fig. 7)***. Press the triangle to the right side to make **Unit 1**. Make 16 Unit 1's.

**Fig. 7**

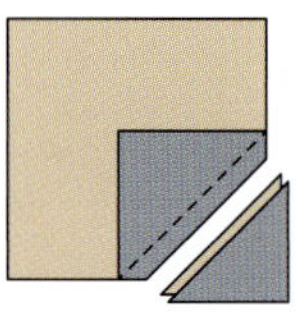

**Unit 1** (make 16)

2. Sew together four light print **squares B**, one blue print **square B**, and four **Unit 1's** to make a **Shoo Fly Block**. Sew the pieces together in rows, pressing the seam allowances toward the squares B. Sew the rows together. Make 4 Shoo Fly Blocks.

**Shoo Fly Block** (make 4)

## ASSEMBLING THE QUILT TOP

*Refer to **Quilt Top Diagram** to assemble quilt top.*

1. Sew the blocks together in rows. Sew the rows together.
2. Using diagonal seams, sew **inner border strips** together to make one continuous strip ***(Fig. 8)***.

**Fig. 8**

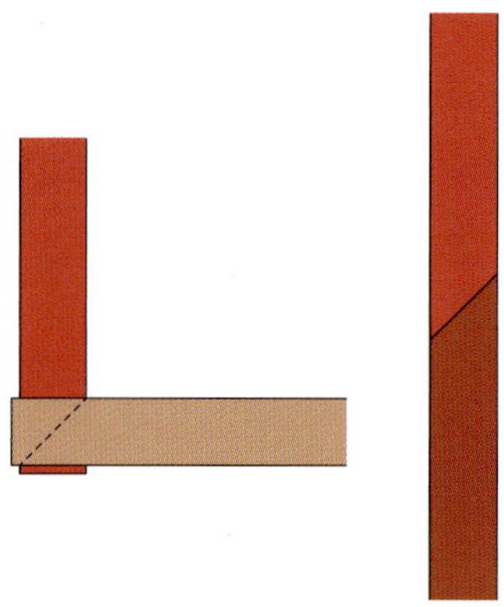

3. Measure *length* across center of quilt top center. Cut 2 **inner side borders** from continuous strip. Matching centers and corners, sew inner side borders to quilt top center.
4. Measure *width* across center of quilt top center (including added borders). Cut 2 **inner top/bottom borders** from continuous strip. Matching centers and corners, sew inner top/bottom borders to quilt top center.
5. Repeat Steps 3-4 to add **outer side**, then **outer top/bottom borders**.

**Quilt Top Diagram**

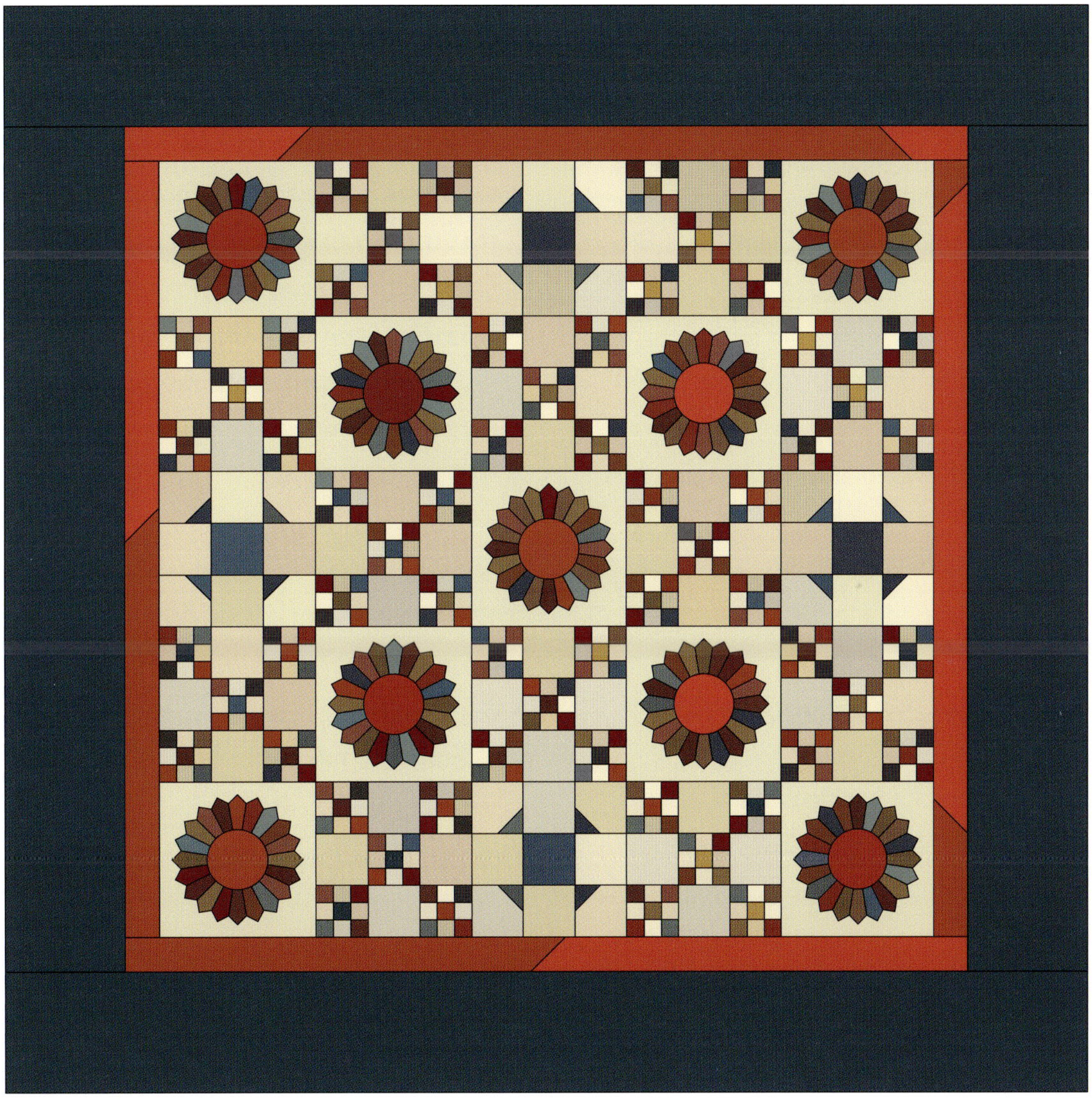

## COMPLETING THE QUILT

1. Follow **Quilting**, page 42, to mark, layer, and quilt as desired. Quilt shown is quilted with feathers around the Prairie Dresden Blocks and along the outer borders and with an all-over leaf design over the remainder of the quilt.
2. Follow **Making a Hanging Sleeve**, page 44, if a hanging sleeve is desired.
3. Sew **binding strips** together end to end diagonally. Follow **Attaching Binding with Mitered Corners**, page 45, to bind quilt.

# DESERT STARS

*The beauty of a Lone Star lies in its radiating color and precise piecing. Study the* ***Lone Star Diamond Point Layout****, page 27, in planning your color selection. Placing two or three fabrics together of the same color family, but of different values - light, medium, dark - will make your star appear to glow. Also keep the color of the background in mind because you will want your star, especially the points, to have a strong contrast. Exercise patience in planning, cutting, and piecing.*

## SHOPPING LIST

*Yardage is based on 43"/44" (109 cm/112 cm) wide fabric with a usable width of 40" (102 cm). Fat quarters are approximately 22" x 18" (56 cm x 46 cm.) It is crucial that you do not stretch or distort the bias edges. We recommend prewashing your fabrics and starching them to prevent this. Liquid starch added to the wash or spray starch work equally well.*

- ☐ 13 assorted fat quarters for Lone Star Center
- ☐ 1¼ yds (1.1 m) of red-orange print fabric for Lone Star Center background
- ☐ 2 yds (1.8 m) of green stripe fabric for borders
- ☐ 1¾ yds (1.6 m) **total** of assorted beige print fabrics for flying geese
- ☐ 2½ yds (2.3 m) of tan print fabric for Star Border Blocks background
- ☐ 5¾ yds (5.3 m) **total** of assorted print fabrics for Star Border Blocks, pieced square borders, and flying geese borders
- ☐ 9 yds (8.2 m) of fabric for backing
- ☐ ⅞ yd (80 cm) **total** of assorted fabrics for binding
- ☐ 108" x 108" (274 cm x 274 cm) piece of batting

## CUTTING THE PIECES

*Follow* ***Rotary Cutting****, page 36, to cut fabric. Cut all strips from the selvage-to-selvage width of the fabric unless otherwise stated. Mitered borders are cut longer than needed and will be trimmed to fit quilt top center. All measurements include ¼" seam allowances.*

### From assorted fat quarters:

- For the Lone Star Center, cut 1½" x 20" strips of the following:
  - 1 **strip** from ***each*** of 2 fat quarters.
  - 2 **strips** from ***each*** of 2 fat quarters.
  - 3 **strips** from ***each*** of 2 fat quarters.
  - 4 **strips** from ***each*** of 2 fat quarters.
  - 5 **strips** from ***each*** of 2 fat quarters.
  - 6 **strips** from ***each*** of 2 fat quarters.
  - 7 **strips** from 1 fat quarter.

### From red-orange print fabric:

- Cut 1 strip 17¼" wide. From this strip, cut 1 square 17¼" x 17¼". Cut square **twice** diagonally to make 4 **triangles B**.
- Cut 2 strips 11⅝" wide. From these strips, cut 4 **squares C** 11⅝" x 11⅝".

### From green stripe fabric:

- Cut 10 strips 2¼" wide. Sew strips together end to end. From the pieced strip, cut:
  - 4 **borders #1** 2¼" x 43".
  - 4 **borders #2** 2¼" x 52½".
- Cut 20 strips 2" wide. Sew strips together end to end. From the pieced strip, cut:
  - 4 **borders #3** 2" x 93".
  - 4 **borders #4** 2" x 102".

**Finished Quilt Size:** 100" x 100" (254 cm x 254 cm)

**Finished Center Star Block Size:** 37" x 37" (94 cm x 94 cm)

**Finished Star Border Block Size:** 10 1/4" x 10 1/4" (26 cm x 26 cm)

**From assorted beige print fabrics:**

- Cut 364 squares 2 3/8" x 2 3/8". Cut each square **once** diagonally to make 728 **triangles E.**

**From tan print fabric:**

- Cut 4 strips 15 3/4" wide. From these strips, cut 8 squares 15 3/4" x 15 3/4". Cut each square **twice** diagonally to make 32 **triangles I.**
- Cut 2 strips 8 1/4" wide. From this strip, cut 8 squares 8 1/4" x 8 1/4". Cut each square **once** diagonally to make 16 **triangles J.**

**From assorted print fabrics:**

- Cut 80 **strips** $1^{1}/_{2}$" x 20" for the star border blocks. (Plan combinations prior to cutting. Note that two matching strips are used for each block.)
- Cut 91 squares $4^{1}/_{4}$" x $4^{1}/_{4}$". Cut each square ***twice*** diagonally to make 364 **triangles D**.
- Cut 216 **squares F** $2^{1}/_{2}$" x $2^{1}/_{2}$".
- Cut 20 sets of 4 matching triangles G and 4 squares H. For triangles G, cut 20 squares $5^{1}/_{2}$" x $5^{1}/_{2}$". Cut each square ***twice*** diagonally to make a **total** of 80 **triangles G**. Cut a **total** of 80 **squares H** $3^{1}/_{2}$" x $3^{1}/_{2}$".

**From binding fabric:**

- Cut assorted **binding strips** $2^{1}/_{4}$" wide in various lengths to total 12 yds when sewn together diagonally end to end.

## MAKING THE LONE STAR CENTER

*Follow **Machine Piecing**, page 37, and **Pressing**, page 39, to make quilt top. Use $^{1}/_{4}$" seam allowances throughout.*

### Piecing the Lone Star Strip Sets

1. Sew together assorted **strips** 1-7, staggering each strip approximately 1" to make **Strip Set A**. Being careful not to stretch or allow the seamlines to curve, press the seam allowances open.

**Strip Set A**

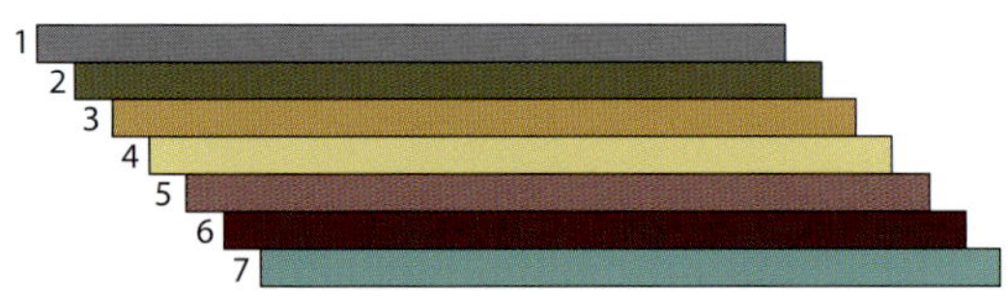


2. Sew together assorted **strips** 2-8, staggering each strip approximately 1" to make **Strip Set B**. Press the seam allowances open.

**Strip Set B**

3. Continue in the same manner to make Strip Sets C through G.

### Cutting the Lone Star Strips

*(**Note:** You may need to correct your angle after you have cut a few strips. To do this, re-align the 45° guideline with the straight edge and cut a new angled edge.)*

1. Using a long rotary cutting ruler, align the 45° guideline with the straight edge of Strip Set A. To make an angled edge from which to measure, cut off the excess fabric at the end of the strips. Cut strips $1^{1}/_{2}$" wide ***(Fig. 1)***. Cut a **total** of eight strips from each of Strip Sets A through G.

**Fig. 1**

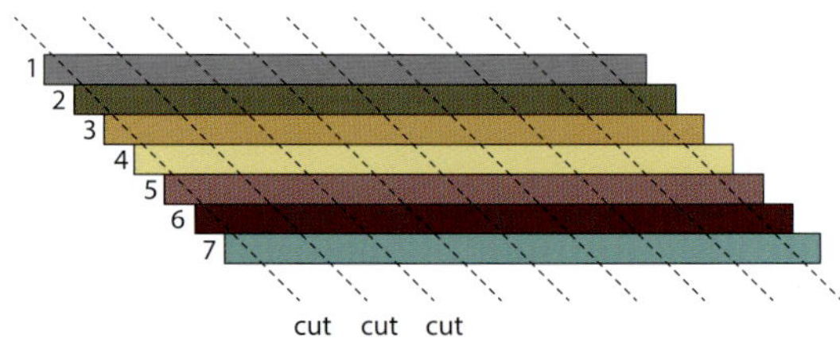


### Assembling the Lone Star Diamond Points

1. Refer to the **Lone Star Diamond Point Layout** to lay out the strips from Strip Set A through G. Being careful to intersect the seamlines at the stitching line, pin two strips together. A small amount of the $^{1}/_{4}$" seam allowance will extend at the ends of each set of strips. Sew together carefully, checking frequently to make sure the seam intersections are accurate. Sew remaining strips together. Press seam allowances open. Make 8 lone star diamond points.

**Lone Star Diamond Point Layout**

(make 8)

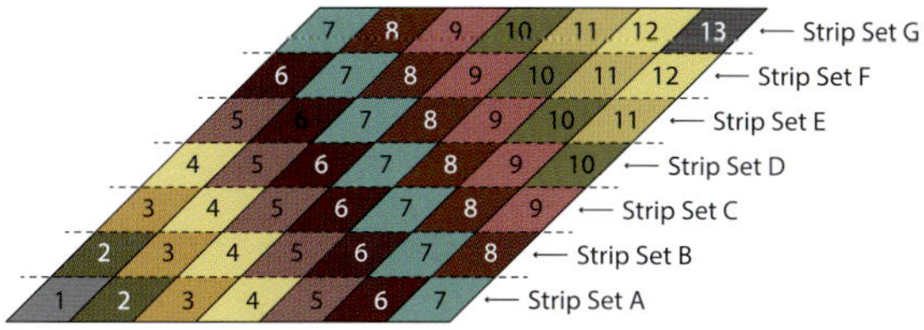


### Assembling the Lone Star Center

*Refer to **Working With Set-In Seams**, page 38.*

1. Join 4 of the diamond points to make half of the star, stitching just to the stitching line at the outer edges. Leave these seam allowances free so that you can set in the red-orange triangles B and squares C. Make 2 half stars. Sew the half stars together to make the complete star.
2. The triangles B and squares C are oversized and will be trimmed after the completion of the center star. Sew 4 **triangles B** to the sides of the star, trimming even with the edge of the diamond points as shown in the **Trimming Diagram**. Sew the 4 **squares C** to the corners of the star.

**Trimming Diagram**

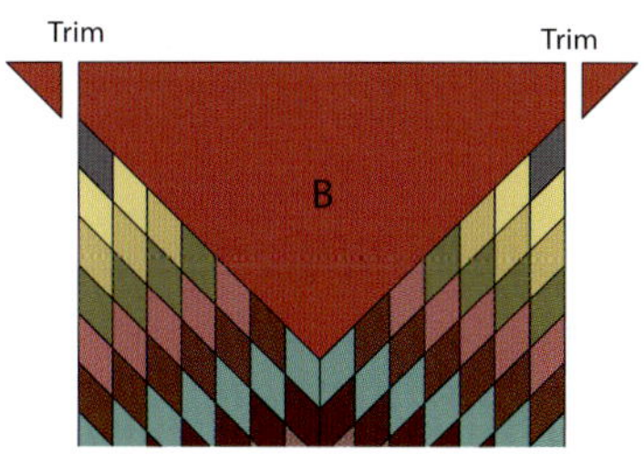


3. Centering star, trim the quilt top center to $37^{1}/_{2}$" x $37^{1}/_{2}$".

## ADDING THE INNER BORDERS

### Flying Geese Border

1. Refer to **Adding Mitered Border**s, page 39, to sew **borders #1** to the quilt. Quilt top center should measure 41" x 41", including the seam allowances.
2. Refer to the **Flying Geese Diagram**, to sew two matching **triangles E** to one **triangle D** to make a **Flying Geese**. Mixing and matching the triangles, make a total of 364 Flying Geese.

**Flying Geese Diagram** (make 364)

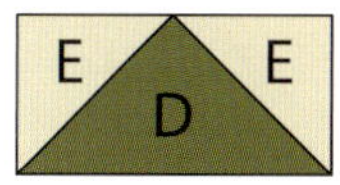


*(**Note:** Before adding the Flying Geese borders, note that the geese point in a counter-clockwise direction.)*

3. Sew 27 Flying Geese together to make the **Top Flying Geese Border**. Sew the border to the top, making sure that the geese point to the left. Repeat for the **Bottom Flying Geese Border**, making sure the geese point to the right.
4. Sew 31 Flying Geese together to make the **Left Flying Geese Border**, turning the top two units so they point in the same direction as the top border. Sew the border to the left side, making sure the geese face downward.
5. Sew 31 Flying Geese together to make the **Right Flying Geese Border**, turning thc bottom two geese so they point in the same direction as the bottom border. Sew the border to the right side, making sure the geese face upward. Quilt top center should measure 47" x 47", including the seam allowances.
6. Refer to **Adding Mitered Border**s to sew **borders #2** to the quilt. Quilt top center should measure $50^{1}/_{2}$" x $50^{1}/_{2}$", including the seam allowances.

**Pieced Square Border**

1. Sew 2 **squares F** together to make a **Unit 1**. Make 108 Unit 1's. Sew 25 Unit 1's together to make the **Top Pieced Square Border**. Sew the Top Pieced Square Border to the top of the quilt. Repeat for the **Bottom Pieced Square Border**.

**Unit 1** (make 108)

2. Sew 29 **Unit 1's** together to make 1 **Side Pieced Square Border**. Make a **total** of 2 Side Pieced Square Borders. Sew the Side Pieced Square Borders to the quilt top. Quilt top center should measure 58½" x 58½", including seam allowances.

## MAKING THE STAR BORDER BLOCKS

1. For each Star Border Block, sew 2 **strips** together to make **Strip Sets H** and **I** in the same manner as the center star. Cut the strip sets into eight 1½" wide strips. Referring to the **Star Border Block Diamond Diagram**, sew the strips together, carefully matching seams. Make a total of 8 diamonds for each block.

**Strip Set H**

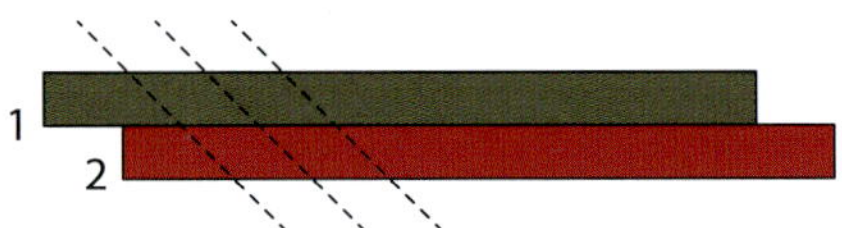


**Strip Set I**

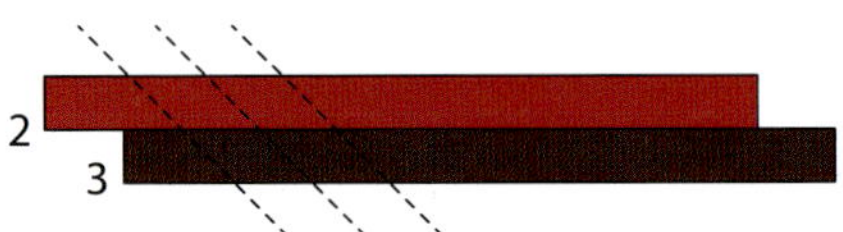


**Star Border Block Diamond Diagram**
(make a total of 8 for each block)

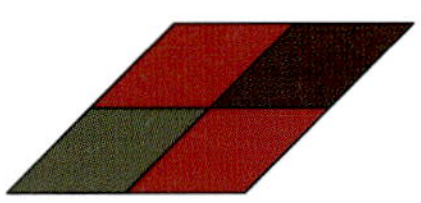

2. Refer to **Star Border Block** to inset **G** and **H** to make a **Star Border Block**. Make 20 blocks.

**Star Border Block** (make 20)

## ADDING THE STAR BLOCK BORDER

*Refer to **Quilt Top Diagram** to assemble quilt top.*

1. To make the top star block border, sew 6 **triangles I**, 4 **triangles J**, and 4 Star Border Blocks together. Repeat to make the bottom star block border. Sew the top and bottom borders to the quilt top. Press seam allowances toward the pieced square border.
2. To make a side star block border, sew 10 **triangles I** and 4 **triangles J** to the sides of 6 Star Border Blocks. Make 2 side star block borders. Sew the side star block borders to the quilt, also pressing toward the pieced square border. Trim quilt top center to measure 87½" x 87½".

## ADDING OUTER BORDERS

1. Refer to **Adding Mitered Borders** to add **borders #3**. Quilt top center should measure 90½" x 90½".
2. *(**Note:** Make sure the Flying Geese in this border point clockwise, which is the opposite direction of the previous Flying Geese Border.)* To make the **Top Flying Geese Border**, sew 60 Flying Geese together. Sew the border to the top of the quilt. Repeat for the **Bottom Flying Geese Border**.

3. To make the **Side Flying Geese Borders**, sew 64 Flying Geese together, turning the end geese units on the bottom of the left border and the top of the right border. Attach borders to sides.

4. Refer to **Adding Mitered Borders** to add **borders #4**.

**Quilt Top Diagram**

## COMPLETING THE QUILT

1. Follow **Quilting**, page 42, to mark, layer, and quilt as desired. For our quilt, all the stars are quilted in the ditch around each diamond. The Lone Star Center and each Star Border Block is quilted with flower motifs and stipple quilting in the backgrounds. Each border and each triangle in the Flying Geese is quilted in the ditch. In the Pieced Square Borders there are three parallel lines through each square. In the Star Border Blocks, small squares or triangles radiate from the center of each background square and triangle.
2. Follow **Making a Hanging Sleeve**, page 44, if a hanging sleeve is desired.
3. Sew **binding strips** together end to end diagonally. Follow **Attaching Binding with Mitered Corners**, page 45, to bind quilt.

# TRAFALGAR SQUARE

## SHOPPING LIST

*Yardage is based on 43"/44" (109 cm/112 cm) wide fabric with a usable width of 40" (102 cm). A fat quarter measures approximately 22" x 18" (53 cm x 46 cm).*

- ☐ fat quarter **each** of four assorted red prints for Night Crossing Blocks, flowers, and circle flower centers
- ☐ fat quarter **each** of two assorted black prints for Night Crossing Blocks
- ☐ fat quarter of black medium scale floral print fabric for Framed Square Block centers and flower centers
- ☐ fat quarter of black and red floral print fabric for Framed Square Block centers and Night Crossing Blocks
- ☐ fat quarter of black, red, and white print fabric for Framed Square Block centers and Night Crossing Blocks
- ☐ 1/2 yd (46 cm) of ivory and black print fabric for Night Crossing Block centers and leaves
- ☐ 3/8 yd (34 cm) of ivory print fabric for Night Crossing Blocks
- ☐ 1/2 yd (46 cm) of red and black stripe fabric for blocks
- ☐ 1/2 yd (46 cm) of black and red stripe fabric for Framed Square Blocks
- ☐ 1/2 yd (46 cm) of ivory and red print fabric for borders #1 and circle flowers
- ☐ 1 1/4 yds (1.1 m) of black and ivory trailing floral print fabric for borders #2 and Night Crossing Blocks
- ☐ 5/8 yd (57 cm) of floral trellis print fabric for borders #3 and Framed Square Block centers
- ☐ 1 3/8 yds (1.3 m) of black, red, and tan small print fabric for borders #4
- ☐ 3/4 yd (69 cm) of black and ivory stripe fabric for Night Crossing Blocks and binding
- ☐ 4 1/2 yds (4.1 m) of fabric for backing
- ☐ 1 1/2 yds (1.4 m) of 17" (43 cm) wide paper-backed fusible web
- ☐ 73" x 81" (185 cm x 206 cm) piece of batting
- ☐ stabilizer

## CUTTING THE PIECES

*Follow **Rotary Cutting**, page 36, to cut fabric. For yardage, cut all strips from the selvage-to-selvage width of the fabric unless otherwise stated. For fat quarters, cut strips parallel to the short edge. Mitered borders are cut longer than needed and will be trimmed to fit quilt top center. All measurements include 1/4" seam allowances.*

### From the four assorted red print fat quarters:

- Cut a **total** of 28 **rectangles E** 1 1/2" x 2 1/2".
- Cut a **total** of 28 **rectangles F** 1 1/2" x 4 1/2".
- Cut a **total** of 28 **rectangles G** 1 1/2" x 6 1/2".

### From the two assorted black print fat quarters:

- Cut a **total** of 18 **rectangles E** 1 1/2" x 2 1/2".
- Cut a **total** of 18 **rectangles F** 1 1/2" x 4 1/2".
- Cut a **total** of 18 **rectangles G** 1 1/2" x 6 1/2".

### From black medium scale floral print fat quarter:

- Cut 4 **squares A** 4 1/2" x 4 1/2".

### From black and red floral print fat quarter:

- Cut 4 **squares A** 4 1/2" x 4 1/2".
- Cut 2 **rectangles E** 1 1/2" x 2 1/2".
- Cut 2 **rectangles F** 1 1/2" x 4 1/2".
- Cut 2 **rectangles G** 1 1/2" x 6 1/2".

**Finished Quilt Size:** 65" x 73" (165 cm x 185 cm)
**Finished Block Size:** 8" x 8" (20 cm x 20 cm)

**From black, red, and white print fat quarter:**

- Cut 4 **squares A** 4$^1/_2$" x 4$^1/_2$".
- Cut 2 **rectangles E** 1$^1/_2$" x 2$^1/_2$".
- Cut 2 **rectangles F** 1$^1/_2$" x 4$^1/_2$".
- Cut 2 **rectangles G** 1$^1/_2$" x 6$^1/_2$".

**From ivory and black print fabric:**

- Cut 15 **squares D** 2$^1/_2$" x 2$^1/_2$".

**From ivory print fabric:**

- Cut 7 strips 1$^1/_2$" wide. From these strips, cut 180 **squares H** 1$^1/_2$" x 1$^1/_2$".

**From red and black stripe fabric:**

- Cut 6 strips 2$^1/_2$" wide. From these strips, cut 16 **rectangles B** 2$^1/_2$" x 4$^1/_2$", 16 **rectangles C** 2$^1/_2$" x 8$^1/_2$", and 4 **corner squares** 2$^1/_2$" x 2$^1/_2$".
- Cut 1 strip 1$^1/_2$" wide. From this strip, cut 2 **rectangles E** 1$^1/_2$" x 2$^1/_2$", 2 **rectangles F** 1$^1/_2$" x 4$^1/_2$", and 2 **rectangles G** 1$^1/_2$" x 6$^1/_2$".

**From black and red stripe fabric:**

- Cut 6 strips 2$^1/_2$" wide. From these strips, cut 14 **rectangles B** 2$^1/_2$" x 4$^1/_2$" and 14 **rectangles C** 2$^1/_2$" x 8$^1/_2$".

**From ivory and red print fabric:**

- Cut 5 strips 2$^1/_2$" wide. Piece these strips together end to end. From this strip, cut 2 **inner side borders #1** 2$^1/_2$" x 48$^1/_2$" and 2 **inner top/bottom borders #1** 2$^1/_2$" x 40$^1/_2$".

**From black and ivory trailing floral fabric:**

- Cut 8 strips 4$^1/_2$" wide. Piece these strips together end to end. From this strip, cut 2 **outer side borders #2** 4$^1/_2$" x 75" and 2 **outer top/bottom borders #2** 4$^1/_2$" x 67".
- Cut 2 strips 1$^1/_2$" wide. From these strips, cut 4 **rectangles E** 1$^1/_2$" x 2$^1/_2$", 4 **rectangles F** 1$^1/_2$" x 4$^1/_2$", and 4 **rectangles G** 1$^1/_2$" x 6$^1/_2$".

**From floral trellis print fabric:**

- Cut 3 **squares A** 4$^1/_2$" x 4$^1/_2$".
- Cut 8 strips 1$^1/_2$" wide. Piece these strips together end to end. From this strip, cut 2 **outer side borders #3** 1$^1/_2$" x 75" and 2 **outer top/bottom borders #3** 1$^1/_2$" x 67".

**From black, red, and tan small print fabric:**

- Cut 8 strips 5$^1/_2$" wide. Piece these strips together end to end. From this strip, cut 2 **outer side borders #4** 5$^1/_2$" x 75" and 2 **outer top/bottom borders #4** 5$^1/_2$" x 67".

**From black and ivory stripe fabric:**

- Cut 2 strips 1$^1/_2$" wide. From these strips, cut 4 **rectangles E** 1$^1/_2$" x 2$^1/_2$", 4 **rectangles F** 1$^1/_2$" x 4$^1/_2$", and 4 **rectangles G** 1$^1/_2$" x 6$^1/_2$".
- Cut 8 **binding strips** 2$^1/_4$" wide.

## PREPARING FUSIBLE APPLIQUÉS

*Appliqué patterns, page 34-35, do not include seam allowances. Follow **Preparing Fusible Appliqués**, page 40, to cut out appliqués.*

**From assorted red print fat quarters:**

- Cut a **total** of 6 **flowers J**.
- Cut a **total** of 8 **circle flower centers M**.

**From black medium scale floral print fat quarter:**

- Cut 6 **flower centers K**.

**From ivory and black print fat quarter:**

- Cut 12 **leaves N**.
- Cut 12 **leaves N** in reverse.

**From ivory and red print fabric:**

- Cut 8 **circle flowers L**.

## MAKING THE FRAMED SQUARE BLOCKS

*Follow* ***Machine Piecing****, page 37, and* ***Pressing****, page 39, to make quilt top. Use 1/4" seam allowances throughout.*

1. Sew a red **rectangle B** to opposite sides of a black **square A**. Press seam allowances away from square A. Sew a red **rectangle C** to the top and bottom. Make a **total** of 8 **Framed Square Block A's**.

**Framed Square Block A** (make 8)

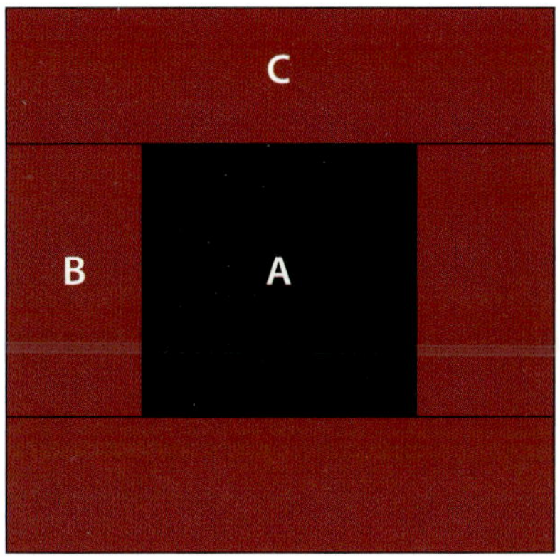


2. Using black **squares A** and black **rectangles B** and **C**, make 7 **Framed Square Block B's**.

**Framed Square Block B** (make 7)

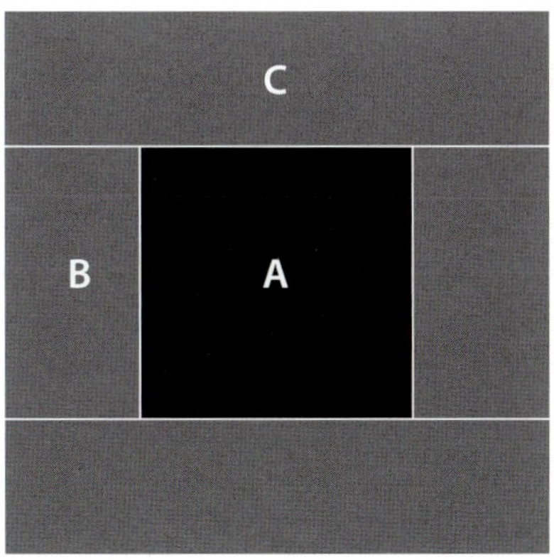


## MAKING THE NIGHT CROSSING BLOCKS

1. Referring to the **Night Crossing Block**, randomly arrange pieces **D** through **H** for a scrappy look. Notice that half of the block contains black fabrics and half of the block contains red fabrics.
2. Sew a **rectangle E** to opposite sides of a **square D**. Press the seam allowances toward the darker fabric.
3. Sew a **square H** to opposite short ends of a **rectangle E**. Make 2. Press the seam allowances toward the darker fabric. Sew these to the top and bottom of the unit made in Step 2.
4. Continue adding rectangles and squares in this manner to make the **Night Crossing Block**. Make a **total** of 15 Night Crossing Blocks.

**Night Crossing Block** (make 15)

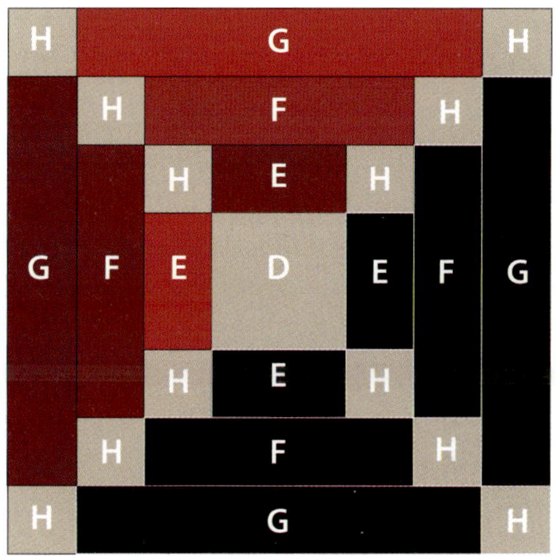


## ASSEMBLING THE QUILT TOP

*Refer to* ***Quilt Top****, page 35, to assemble quilt top.*

### Inner Borders

1. Alternating the blocks, sew the blocks together in rows. Sew the rows together.
2. Sew the **inner side border #1's** to the quilt top. Sew a **corner square** to the short ends of the **inner top/ bottom border #1's** to quilt top. Press the seam allowances toward the ivory and red print fabric.
3. Sew the **inner top/bottom border #1's** to the quilt top.

### Outer Borders

1. For outer side border, match the centers and sew 1 **outer side border #2**, 1 **outer side border #3**, and 1 **outer side border #4** together. Press the seam allowances toward the narrow border strip. Make 2 **outer side borders**.
2. Repeat Step 1 using **outer top/bottom borders** to make 2 **outer top/bottom borders**.
3. Referring to **Quilt Top** for placement, position appliqués on border and fuse in place. Follow **Zigzag Stitch Appliqué**, page 40, to add appliqués to quilt top. Note that you will not be able to position the corner flowers until after the borders are sewn to the quilt.
4. Refer to **Adding Mitered Borders**, page 39, to add outer side, top, and bottom borders to quilt top.
5. Fuse and appliqué the corner flowers on the borders.

## COMPLETING THE QUILT

1. Follow **Quilting**, page 42, to mark, layer, and quilt as desired. Quilt shown is quilted in the ditch along each border and with a feather design in the quilt top center and in each wide border. There is meandering quilting in the inner borders.
2. Follow **Making a Hanging Sleeve**, page 44, if a hanging sleeve is desired.
3. Sew **binding strips** together end to end diagonally. Follow **Attaching Binding with Mitered Corners**, page 45, to bind quilt.

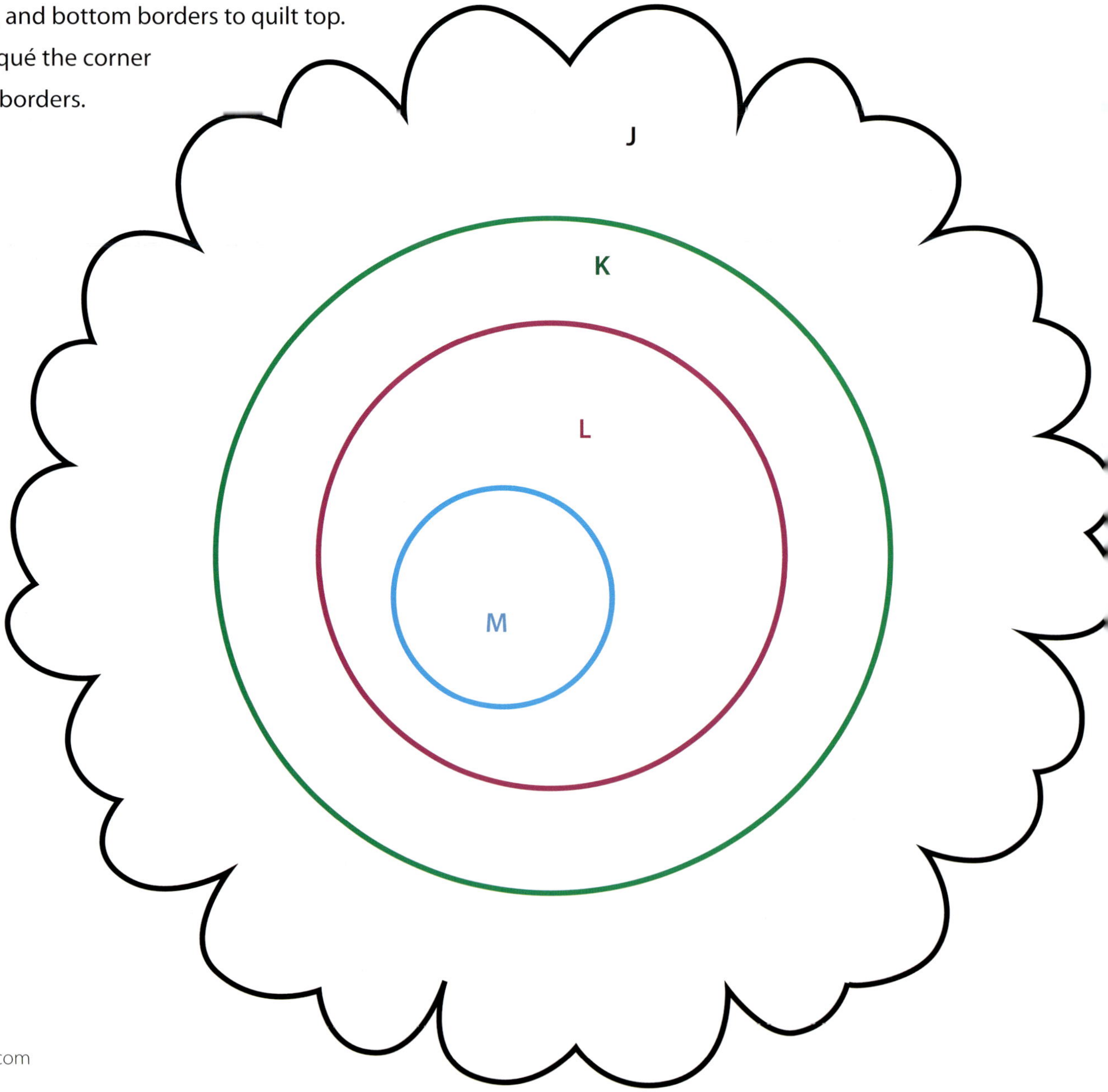

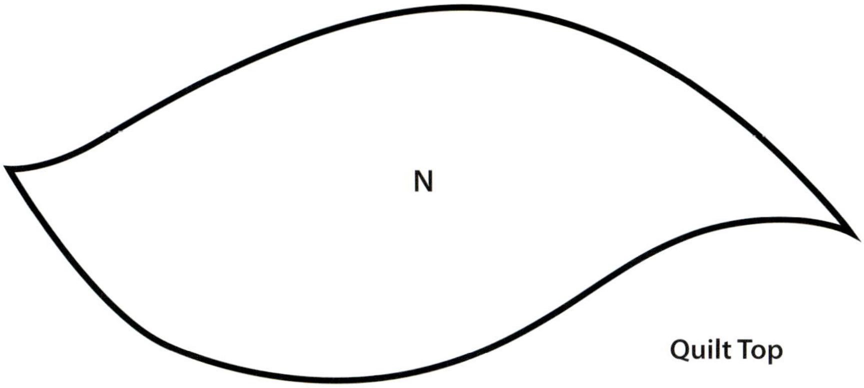


Quilt Top

# GENERAL INSTRUCTIONS

*To make your quilting easier and more enjoyable, we encourage you to carefully read all of the general instructions, study the color photographs, and familiarize yourself with the individual project instructions before beginning a project.*

## FABRICS

### SELECTING FABRICS

Choose high-quality, medium-weight 100% cotton fabrics. All-cotton fabrics hold a crease better, fray less, and are easier to quilt than cotton/polyester blends.

Yardage requirements listed for each project are based on 43"/44" wide fabric with a "usable" width of 40" after shrinkage and trimming selvages. Actual usable width will probably vary slightly from fabric to fabric. Our recommended yardage lengths should be adequate for occasional re-squaring of fabric when many cuts are required.

### PREPARING FABRICS

Pre-washing fabrics may cause edges to ravel. As a result, your fat quarters may not be large enough to cut all of the pieces required for your chosen project. Therefore, we do not recommend pre-washing yardage or fat quarters unless otherwise indicated in project instructions.

Before cutting, prepare fabrics with a steam iron set on cotton and starch or sizing. The starch or sizing will give the fabric a crisp finish. This will make cutting more accurate and may make piecing easier.

## ROTARY CUTTING

### CUTTING FROM YARDAGE

- Place fabric on work surface with fold closest to you.
- Cut all strips from the selvage-to-selvage width of the fabric unless otherwise indicated in project instructions.
- Square left edge of fabric using rotary cutter and rulers *(Figs. 1-2)*.

**Fig. 1**

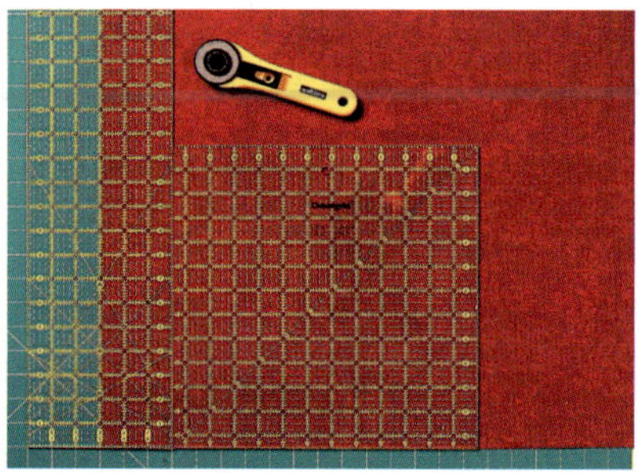

**Fig. 2**

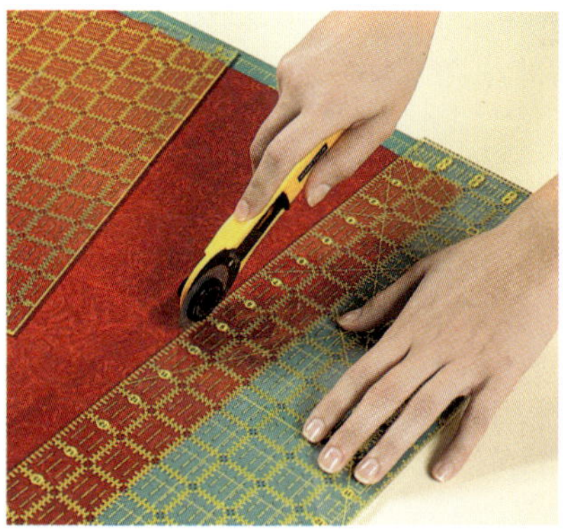

- To cut each strip required for a project, place ruler over cut edge of fabric, aligning desired marking on ruler with cut edge; make cut *(Fig. 3)*.

Fig. 3

- When cutting several strips from a single piece of fabric, it is important to make sure that cuts remain at a perfect right angle to the fold; square fabric as needed.

## CUTTING FROM FAT QUARTERS

- Cut all strips parallel to the edge of the fabric indicated in the project instructions in the same manner as cutting from yardage.

- To cut each strip, place ruler over cut edge of fabric, aligning desired marking on ruler with cut edge; make cut.

# MACHINE PIECING

Precise cutting, followed by accurate piecing, will ensure that all pieces of quilt top fit together well.

- Set sewing machine stitch length for approximately 11 stitches per inch.

- Use neutral-colored general-purpose sewing thread (not quilting thread) in needle and in bobbin.

- An accurate $^{1}/_{4}$" seam allowance is essential. Presser feet that are $^{1}/_{4}$" wide are available for most sewing machines.

- When piecing, always place pieces right sides together and match raw edges; pin if necessary.

- Chain piecing saves time and will usually result in more accurate piecing.

- Trim away points of seam allowances that extend beyond edges of sewn pieces.

## SEWING STRIP SETS

When there are several strips to assemble into a strip set, first sew strips together into pairs, then sew pairs together to form strip set. To help avoid distortion, sew seams in opposite directions *(Fig. 4)*.

Fig. 4

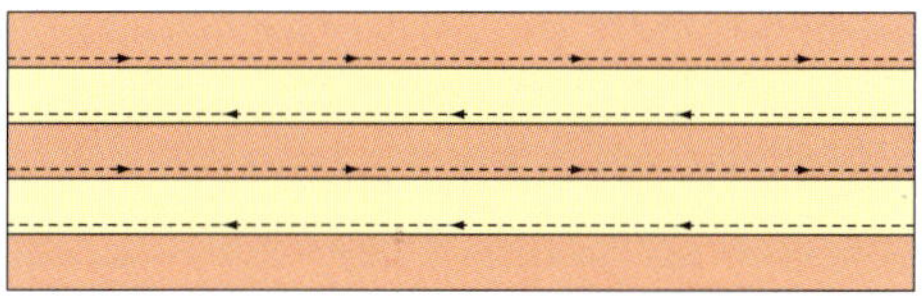

## SEWING ACROSS SEAM INTERSECTIONS

When sewing across intersection of two seams, place pieces right sides together and match seams exactly, making sure seam allowances are pressed in opposite directions *(Fig. 5)*.

Fig. 5

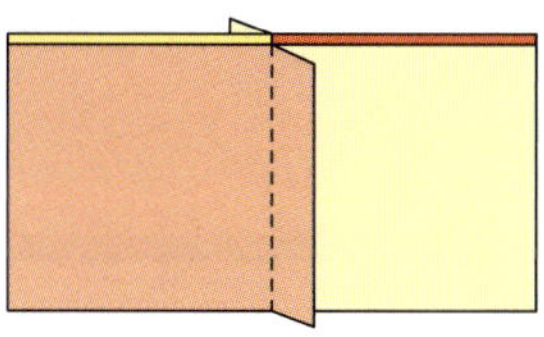

## SEWING SHARP POINTS

To ensure sharp points when joining triangular or diagonal pieces, stitch across the center of the "X" (shown in pink) formed on wrong side by previous seams *(Fig. 6)*.

Fig. 6

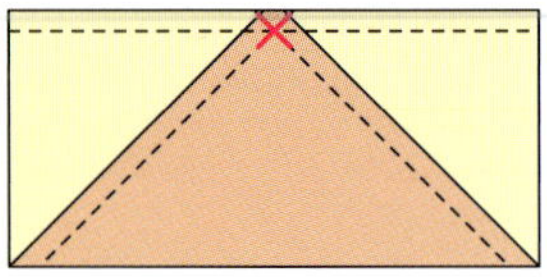

## WORKING WITH SET-IN SEAMS

1. When sewing two diamond or parallelogram pieces together, place pieces right sides together, carefully matching edges; pin. Mark a small dot 1/4" from corner of one piece as shown in Fig. 7. Stitch pieces together in direction shown, stopping at center of dot and backstitching.

Fig. 7

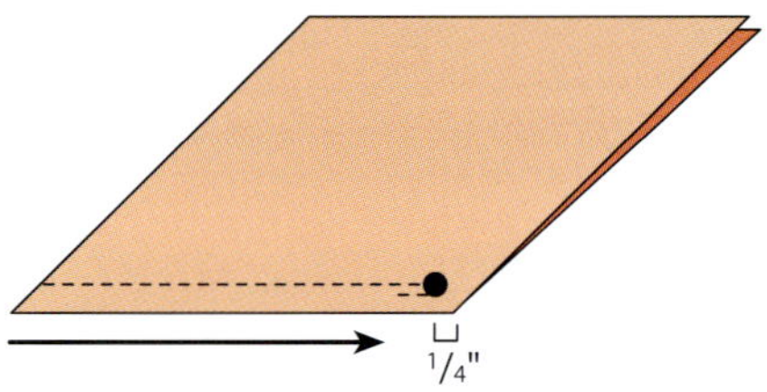


2. For best results, add side triangles, then corner squares to diamond or parallelogram sections. Mark corner of each piece to be set in with a small dot *(Fig. 8)*.

Fig. 8

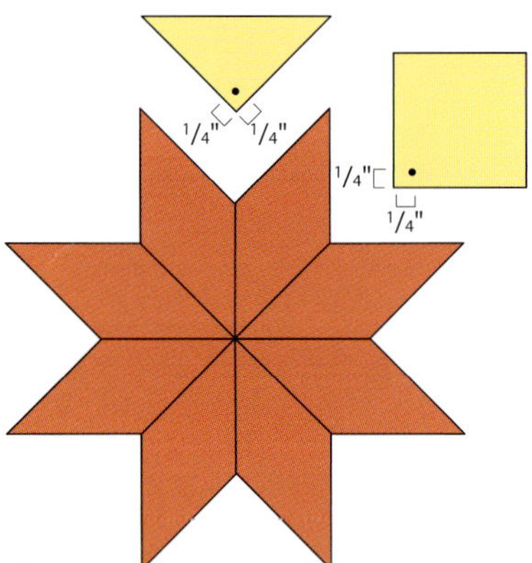


3. To sew first seam, match right sides and pin triangle or square to diamond or parallelogram on the left. Stitch seam from outer edge to dot, backstitching at dot; clip threads *(Fig. 9)*.

Fig. 9

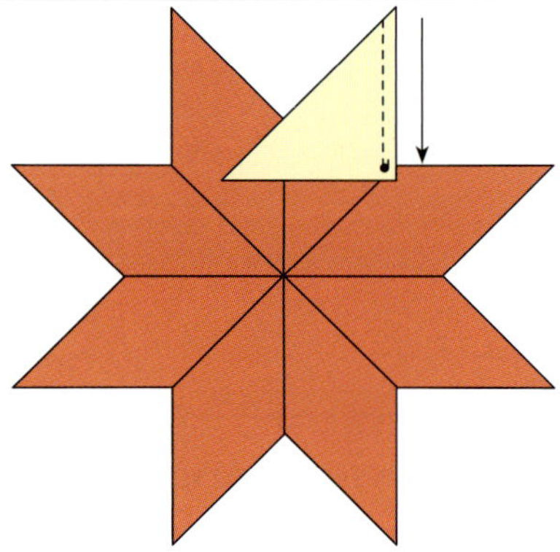

4. To sew second seam, pivot added triangle or square to match raw edges of next diamond or parallelogram. Beginning at dot, take two or three stitches, then backstitch, making sure not to backstitch into previous seam allowance. Continue stitching to outer edge *(Fig. 10)*.

Fig. 10

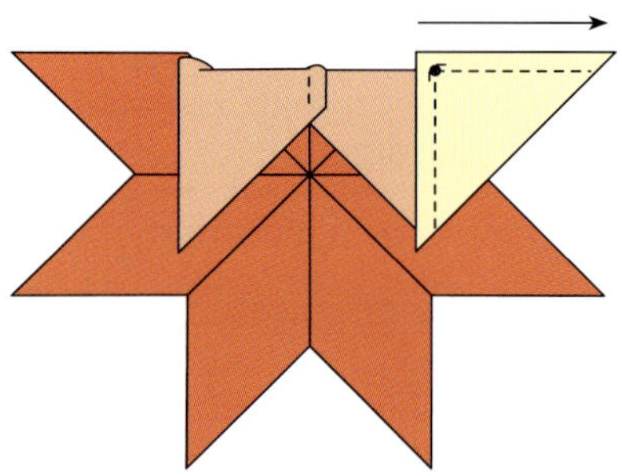

## PRESSING

- Use steam iron set on "Cotton" for all pressing.
- Press after sewing each seam.
- Seam allowances are almost always pressed to one side, usually toward the darker fabric. However, to reduce bulk it may occasionally be necessary to press seam allowances toward the lighter fabric or even to press them open.
- To prevent a dark fabric seam allowance from showing through light fabric, trim the darker seam allowance slightly narrower than the lighter seam allowance.
- To press long seams, such as those in long strip sets, without curving or other distortion, lay strips across width of the ironing board.
- When sewing blocks into rows, seam allowances may be pressed in one direction in odd numbered rows and in the opposite direction in even numbered rows. When sewing rows together, press seam allowances in one direction.

## ADDING MITERED BORDERS

1. Mark the center of each edge of quilt top.
2. Mark center of 1 long edge of top border. Measure across center of quilt top. Matching center marks and raw edges, pin border to center of quilt top edge. From center of border, measure out 1/2 the width of the quilt top in both directions and mark. Match marks on border with corners of quilt top and pin. Easing in any fullness, pin border to quilt top between center and corners. Sew border to quilt top, beginning and ending seams exactly 1/4" from each corner of quilt top and backstitching at beginning and end of stitching *(Fig. 11)*.

Fig. 11

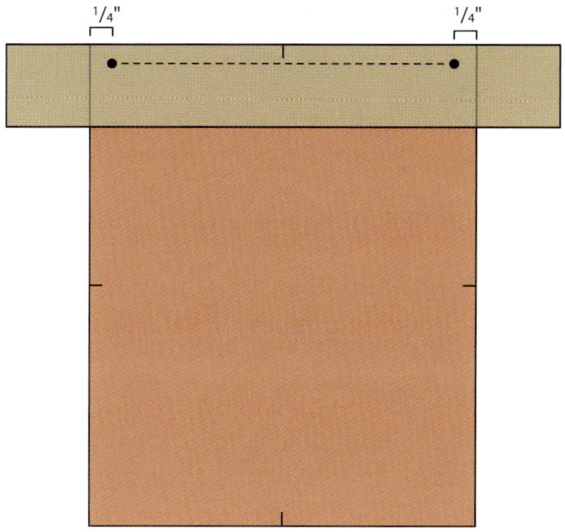


3. Repeat Step 2 to sew bottom, then side borders, to center section of quilt top. To temporarily move first 2 borders out of the way, fold and pin ends as shown in Fig. 12.

Fig. 12

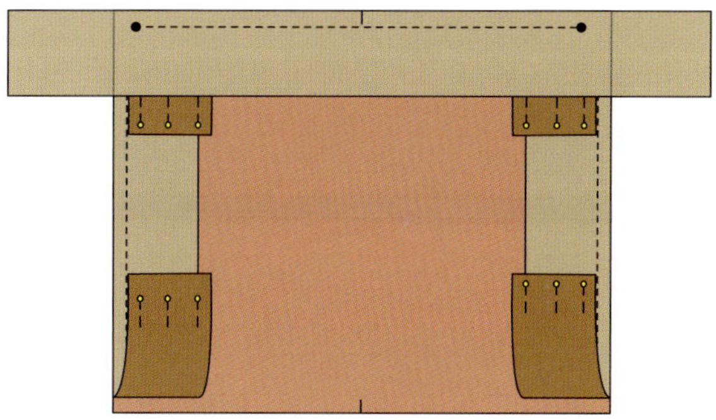

4. Fold 1 corner of the quilt top diagonally with right sides together; use rotary cutting ruler to mark stitching line as shown in **Fig. 13**. Pin borders together along drawn line. Sew on drawn line, backstitching at beginning and end of stitching *(Fig. 14)*.

**Fig. 13**

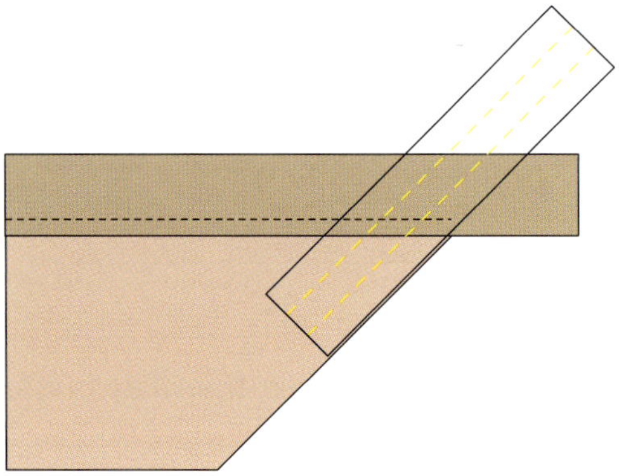

**Fig. 14**

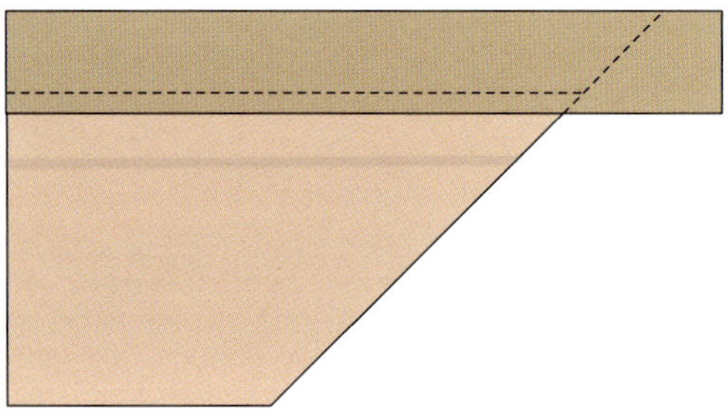

5. Turn mitered corner right side up. Check to see that there is not a gap at the inner end of the seam and that the corner does not pucker.
6. Trim seam allowances to 1/4"; press to one side.
7. Repeat Steps 4-6 to miter each remaining corner.

# MACHINE APPLIQUÉ

## PREPARING FUSIBLE APPLIQUÉS

White or light-colored fabrics may need to be lined with fusible interfacing before applying fusible web to prevent darker fabrics from showing through.

1. Place paper-backed fusible web, paper side up, over appliqué pattern. Trace pattern onto paper side of web with pencil as many times as indicated in project instructions for a single fabric. To reverse a pattern, use a black fine-point marker to trace the pattern onto plain white paper. Flip the paper over and trace the pattern onto the paper side of the fusible web from the "wrong" side of the plain white paper.
2. Follow manufacturer's instructions to fuse traced patterns to wrong side of fabrics. Do not remove paper backing.
3. Use scissors to cut out appliqué pieces along traced lines. Remove paper backing from all pieces.

## ZIGZAG STITCH APPLIQUÉ

The exposed raw edges of the fused appliqué pieces in this book are finished with zigzag stitching using a medium stitch length and a medium stitch width.

1. Pin stabilizer, such as paper or any of the commercially available products, on wrong side of background fabric before stitching appliqués in place.
2. Thread sewing machine with general-purpose thread; use general-purpose thread that matches background fabric in bobbin.
3. Set sewing machine for a medium (approximately 1/8") zigzag stitch and a medium stitch length. Slightly loosening the top tension may yield a smoother stitch.

4. Begin by stitching two or three stitches in place (drop feed dogs or set stitch length at 0) to anchor thread. Most of the zigzag stitch should be on the appliqué with the right edge of the stitch falling at the outside edge of the appliqué. Stitch over all exposed raw edges of appliqué pieces.
5. (**Note**: Dots on **Figs. 15-20** indicate where to leave needle in fabric when pivoting.) For outside corners, stitch just past corner, stopping with needle in background fabric *(Fig. 15)*. Raise presser foot. Pivot project, lower presser foot, and stitch adjacent side *(Fig. 16)*.

**Fig. 15**

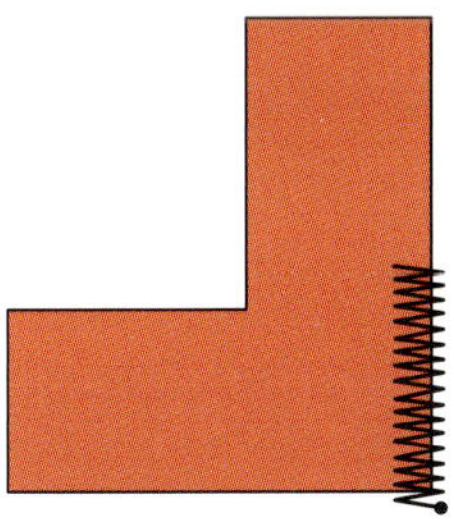

**Fig. 16**

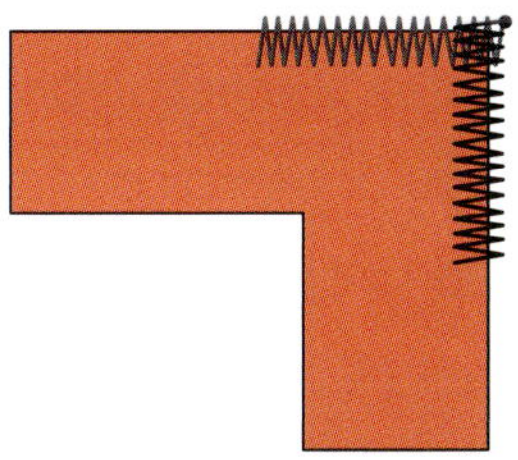

6. For inside corners, stitch just past corner, stopping with needle in appliqué fabric *(Fig. 17)*. Raise presser foot. Pivot project, lower presser foot, and stitch adjacent side *(Fig. 18)*.

**Fig. 17**

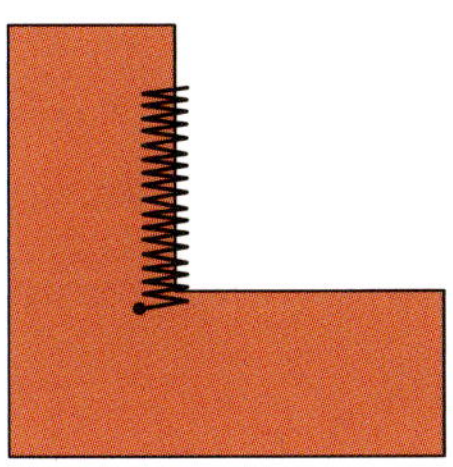

**Fig. 18**

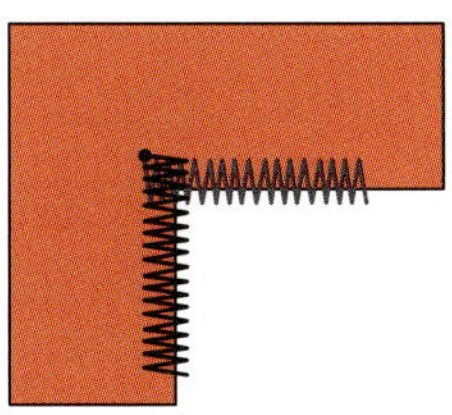

7. When stitching outside curves, stop with needle in background fabric. Raise presser foot and pivot project as needed. Lower presser foot and continue stitching, pivoting as often as necessary to follow curve *(Fig. 19)*.

**Fig. 19**

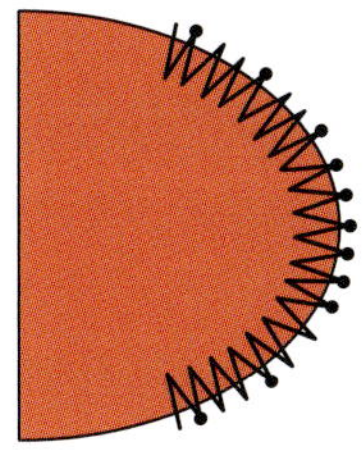

8. When stitching inside curves, stop with needle in appliqué fabric. Raise presser foot and pivot project as needed. Lower presser foot and continue stitching, pivoting as often as necessary to follow curve *(Fig. 20)*.

**Fig. 20**

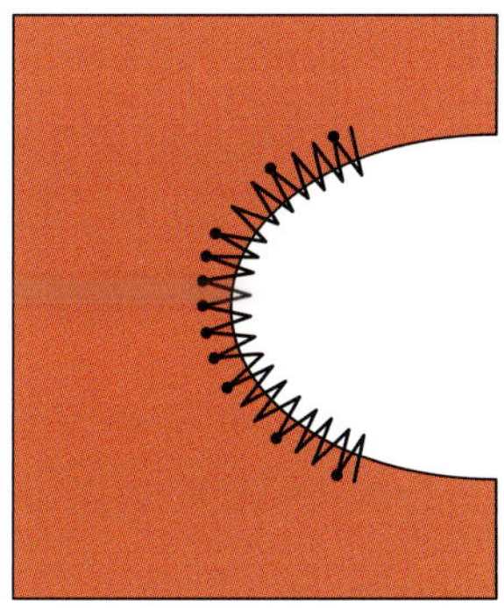

9. Do not backstitch at end of stitching. Pull threads to wrong side of background fabric; knot thread and trim ends.
10. Carefully tear away stabilizer.

## QUILTING

Quilting holds the three layers (top, batting, and backing) of the quilt together and can be done by hand or machine. Because marking, layering, and quilting are interrelated and may be done in different orders depending on circumstances, please read entire Quilting section, pages 42-44, before beginning project.

### TYPES OF QUILTING DESIGNS

#### In the Ditch Quilting

Quilting along seamlines or along edges of appliquéd pieces is called "in the ditch" quilting. This type of quilting should be done on side opposite the seam allowance and does not have to be marked.

#### Outline Quilting

Quilting a consistent distance, usually 1/4", from seam or appliqué is called "outline" quilting. Outline quilting may be marked, or 1/4" masking tape may be placed along seamlines for quilting guide. (Do not leave tape on quilt longer than necessary, since it may leave an adhesive residue.)

#### Motif Quilting

Quilting a design, such as a feathered wreath, is called "motif" quilting. This type of quilting should be marked before basting quilt layers together.

#### Echo Quilting

Quilting that follows the outline of an appliquéd or pieced design with two or more parallel lines is called "echo" quilting. This type of quilting does not need to be marked.

#### Channel Quilting

Quilting with straight, parallel lines is called "channel" quilting. This type of quilting may be marked or stitched using a guide.

#### Crosshatch Quilting

Quilting straight lines in a grid pattern is called "crosshatch" quilting. Lines may be stitched parallel to edges of quilt or stitched diagonally. This type of quilting may be marked or stitched using a guide.

#### Meandering Quilting

Quilting in random curved lines and swirls is called "meandering" quilting. Quilting lines should not cross or touch each other. This type of quilting does not need to be marked.

#### Stipple Quilting

Meandering quilting that is very closely spaced is called "stipple" quilting. Stippling will flatten the area quilted and is often stitched in background areas to raise appliquéd or pieced designs. This type of quilting does not need to be marked.

### MARKING QUILTING LINES

Quilting lines may be marked using fabric marking pencils, chalk markers, or water- or air-soluble pens.

Simple quilting designs may be marked with chalk or chalk pencil after basting. A small area may be marked, then quilted, before moving to next area to be marked. Intricate designs should be marked before basting using a more durable marker.

***Caution:*** *Pressing may permanently set some marks. Test different markers on scrap fabric to find one that marks clearly and can be thoroughly removed.*

A wide variety of pre-cut quilting stencils, as well as entire books of quilting patterns, are available. Using a stencil makes it easier to mark intricate or repetitive designs.

To make a stencil from a pattern, center template plastic over pattern and use a permanent marker to trace pattern onto plastic. Use a craft knife with single or double blade to cut channels along traced lines *(Fig. 21)*.

Fig. 21

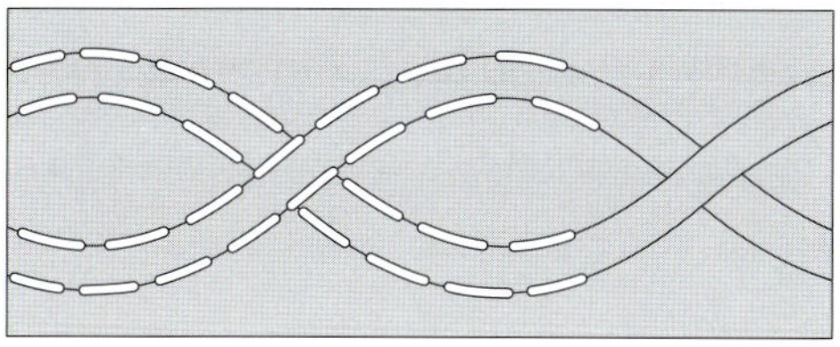

## PREPARING THE BACKING

To allow for slight shifting of quilt top during quilting, backing should be approximately 4" larger on all sides. Yardage requirements listed for quilt backings are calculated for 43"/44"w fabric with a usable width of 40". Using 90"w or 108"w fabric for the backing of a bed-sized quilt may eliminate piecing. To piece a backing using 43"/44"w fabric, use the following instructions.

1. Measure length and width of quilt top; add 8" to each measurement.
2. If determined width is 79" or less, cut backing fabric into two lengths slightly longer than determined length measurement. Trim selvages. Place lengths with right sides facing and sew long edges together, forming a tube *(Fig. 22)*. Match seams and press along one fold *(Fig. 23)*. Cut along pressed fold to form single piece *(Fig. 24)*.

Fig. 22

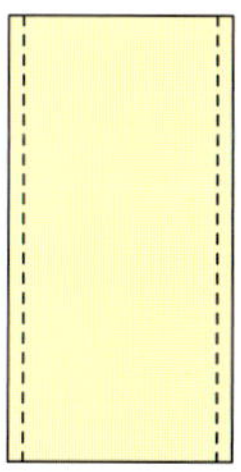

Fig. 23

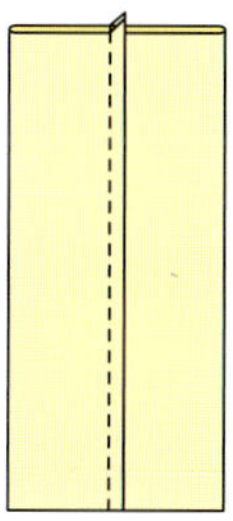

Fig. 24

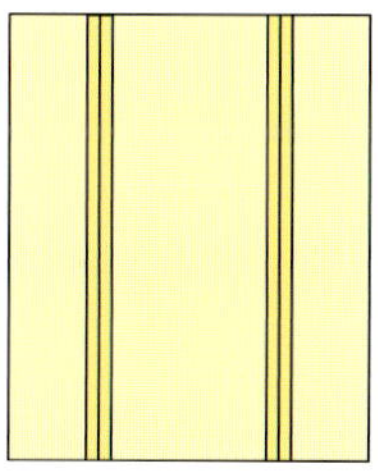

3. If determined width is more than 79", it may require less fabric yardage if the backing is pieced horizontally. Divide determined length measurement by 40" to determine how many widths will be needed. Cut required number of widths the determined width measurement. Trim selvages. Sew long edges together to form single piece.
4. Trim backing to size determined in Step 1; press seam allowances open.

## CHOOSING THE BATTING

The appropriate batting will make quilting easier. For fine hand quilting, choose low-loft batting. All cotton or cotton/polyester blend battings work well for machine quilting because the cotton helps "grip" quilt layers. If quilt is to be tied, a high-loft batting, sometimes called extra-loft or fat batting, may be used to make quilt "fluffy."

Types of batting include cotton, polyester, wool, cotton/polyester blend, cotton/wool blend, and silk.

When selecting batting, refer to package labels for characteristics and care instructions. Cut batting same size as prepared backing.

## ASSEMBLING THE QUILT

1. Examine wrong side of quilt top closely; trim any seam allowances and clip any threads that may show through front of the quilt. Press quilt top, being careful not to "set" any marked quilting lines.
2. Place backing wrong side up on flat surface. Use masking tape to tape edges of backing to surface. Place batting on top of backing fabric. Smooth batting gently, being careful not to stretch or tear. Center quilt top right side up on batting.

3. Use 1" rustproof safety pins to "pin-baste" all layers together, spacing pins approximately 4" apart. Begin at center and work toward outer edges to secure all layers. If possible, place pins away from areas that will be quilted, although pins may be removed as needed when quilting.

## MACHINE QUILTING METHODS

Use general-purpose thread in bobbin. Do not use quilting thread. Thread the needle of machine with general-purpose thread or transparent monofilament thread to make quilting blend with quilt top fabrics. Use decorative thread, such as a metallic or contrasting-color general-purpose thread, to make quilting lines stand out more.

### Straight-Line Quilting

The term "straight-line" is somewhat deceptive, since curves (especially gentle ones) as well as straight lines can be stitched with this technique.

1. Set stitch length for six to ten stitches per inch and attach walking foot to sewing machine.
2. Determine which section of quilt will have longest continuous quilting line, oftentimes area from center top to center bottom. Roll up and secure each edge of quilt to help reduce the bulk, keeping fabrics smooth. Smaller projects may not need to be rolled.
3. Begin stitching on longest quilting line, using very short stitches for the first 1/4" to "lock" quilting. Stitch across project, using one hand on each side of walking foot to slightly spread fabric and to guide fabric through machine. Lock stitches at end of quilting line.
4. Continue machine quilting, stitching longer quilting lines first to stabilize quilt before moving on to other areas.

### Free-Motion Quilting

Free-motion quilting may be free form or may follow a marked pattern.

1. Attach darning foot to sewing machine and lower or cover feed dogs.
2. Position quilt under darning foot; lower foot. Holding top thread, take a stitch and pull bobbin thread to top of quilt. To "lock" beginning of quilting line, hold top and bobbin threads while making three to five stitches in place.
3. Use one hand on each side of darning foot to slightly spread fabric and to move fabric through the machine. Even stitch length is achieved by using smooth, flowing hand motion and steady machine speed. Slow machine speed and fast hand movement will create long stitches. Fast machine speed and slow hand movement will create short stitches. Move quilt sideways, back and forth, in a circular motion, or in a random motion to create desired designs; do not rotate quilt. Lock stitches at end of each quilting line.

## MAKING A HANGING SLEEVE

Attaching a hanging sleeve to back of wall hanging or quilt before the binding is added allows project to be displayed on wall.

1. Measure width of quilt top edge and subtract 1". Cut piece of fabric 7"w by determined measurement.
2. Press short edges of fabric piece 1/4" to wrong side; press edges 1/4" to wrong side again and machine stitch in place.
3. Matching wrong sides, fold piece in half lengthwise to form a tube.
4. Follow project instructions to sew binding to quilt top and to trim backing and batting. Before Blindstitching binding to backing, match raw edges and stitch hanging sleeve to center top edge on back of quilt.

5. Finish binding quilt, treating hanging sleeve as part of backing.
6. Blindstitch bottom of hanging sleeve to backing, taking care not to stitch through to front of quilt.
7. Insert dowel or slat into hanging sleeve.

## ATTACHING BINDING WITH MITERED CORNERS

1. Matching wrong sides and raw edges, press strip(s) in half lengthwise to complete binding.
2. Beginning with one end near center on bottom edge of quilt, lay binding around quilt to make sure that seams in binding will not end up at a corner. Adjust placement if necessary. Matching raw edges of binding to raw edge of quilt top, pin binding to right side of quilt along one edge.
3. When you reach first corner, mark 1/4" from corner of quilt top *(Fig. 25)*.

Fig. 25

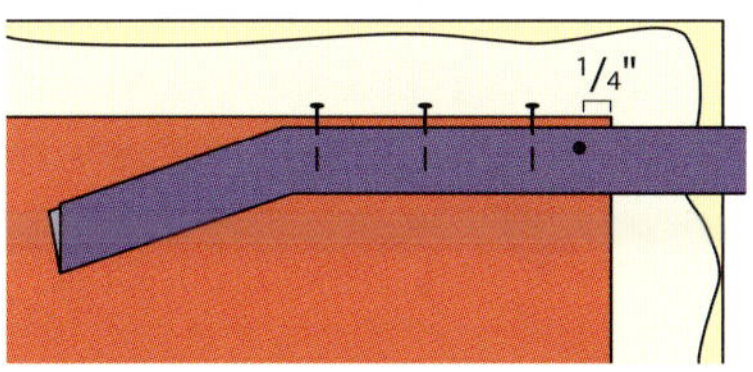


4. Beginning approximately 10" from end of binding and using 1/4" seam allowance, sew binding to quilt, backstitching at beginning of stitching and at mark *(Fig. 26)*. Lift needle out of fabric and clip thread.

Fig. 26

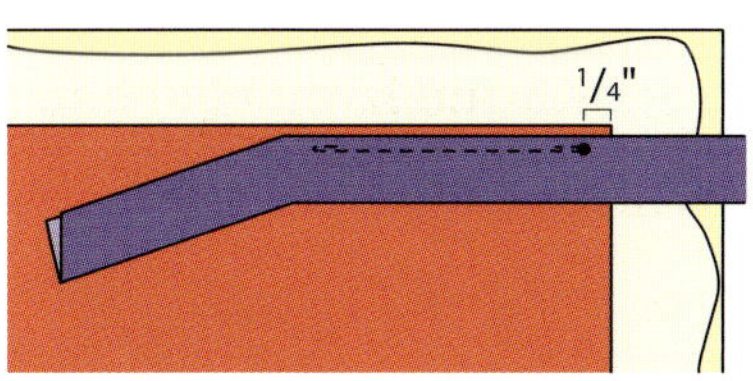


5. Fold binding as shown in **Figs. 27-28** and pin binding to adjacent side, matching raw edges. When you've reached the next corner, mark 1/4" from edge of quilt top.

Fig. 27

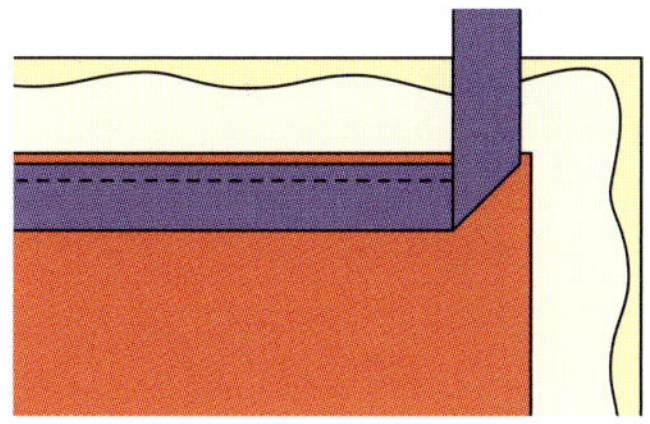

Fig. 28

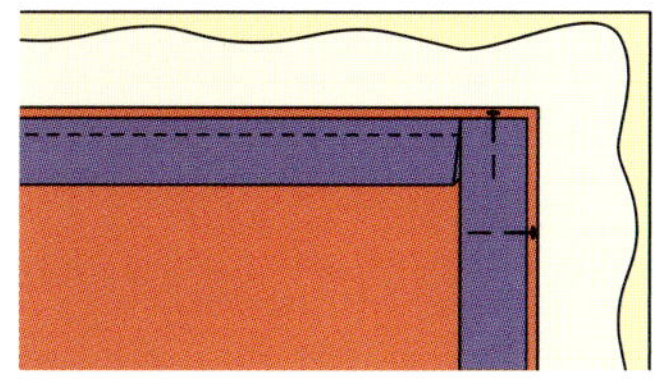

6. Backstitching at edge of quilt top, sew pinned binding to quilt *(Fig. 29)*; backstitch at the next mark. Lift needle out of fabric and clip thread.

Fig. 29

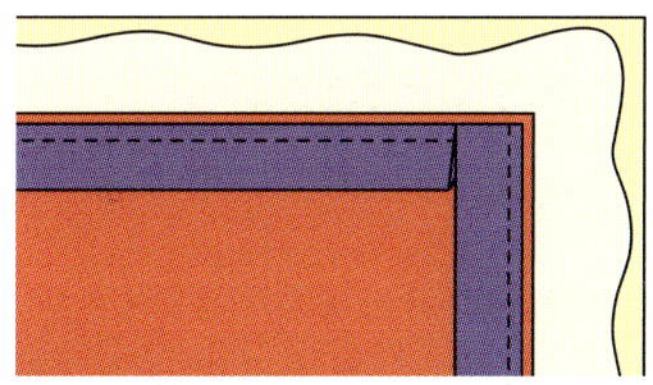

7. Continue sewing binding to quilt, stopping approximately 10" from starting point *(Fig. 30)*.

Fig. 30

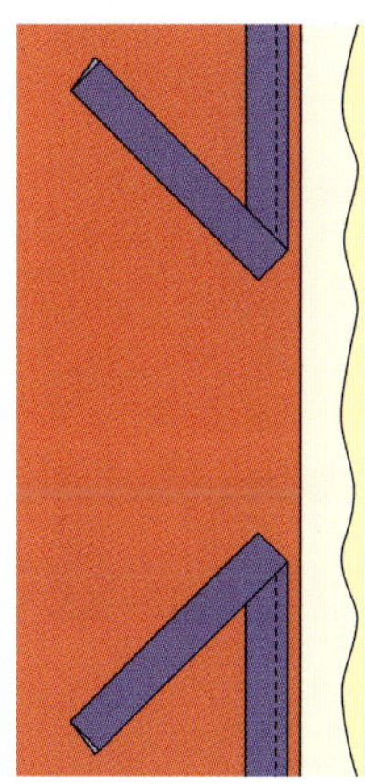

8. Bring beginning and end of binding to center of opening and fold each end back, leaving a $^1/_4$" space between folds *(Fig. 31)*. Finger press folds.

Fig. 31

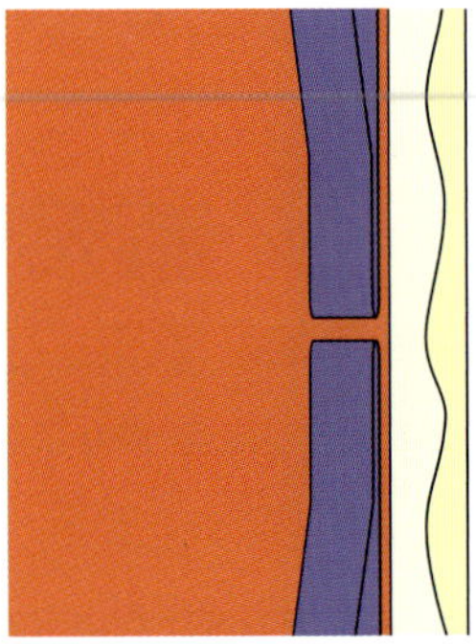

9. Unfold ends of binding and draw a line across wrong side in finger-pressed crease. Draw a line through the lengthwise pressed fold of binding at the same spot to create a cross mark. With edge of ruler at cross mark, line up 45˚ angle marking on ruler with one long side of binding. Draw a diagonal line from edge to edge. Repeat on remaining end, making sure that the two diagonal lines are angled the same way *(Fig. 32)*.

Fig. 32

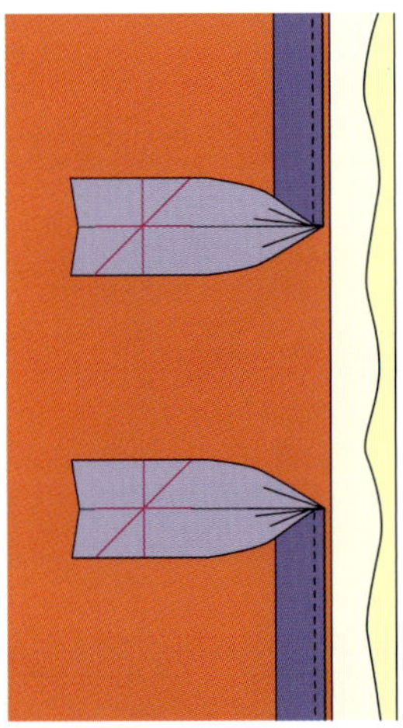

10. Matching right sides and diagonal lines, pin binding ends together at right angles *(Fig. 33)*.

Fig. 33

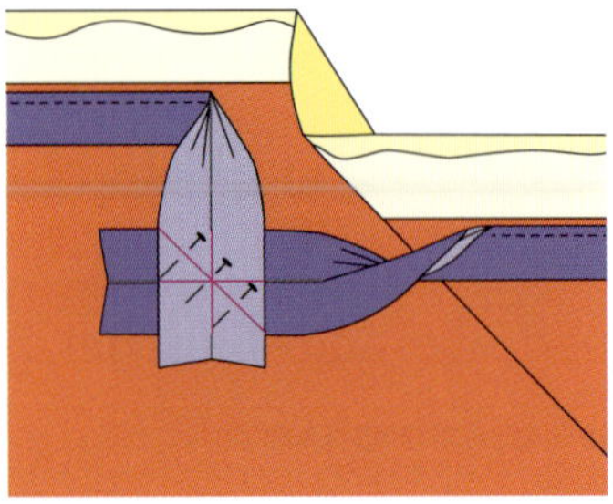

11. Machine stitch along diagonal line *(Fig. 34)*, removing pins as you stitch.

Fig. 34

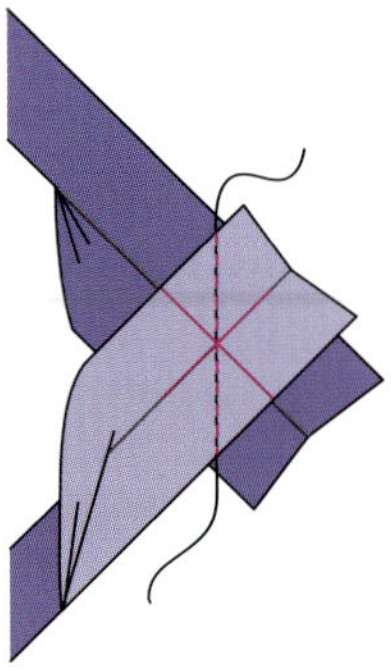

12. Lay binding against quilt to double check that it is correct length.
13. Trim binding ends, leaving $^1/_4$" seam allowances; press seam allowances open. Stitch binding to quilt.
14. If using $2^1/_2$"w binding (finished size $^1/_2$"), trim backing and batting a scant $^1/_4$" larger than quilt top so that batting and backing will fill the binding when it is folded over to quilt backing. If using narrower binding, trim backing and batting even with edges of quilt top.

**15.** On one edge of quilt, fold binding over to quilt backing and pin pressed edge in place, covering stitching line *(Fig. 35)*. On adjacent side, fold binding over, forming a mitered corner *(Fig. 36)*. Repeat to pin remainder of binding in place.

Fig. 35

Fig. 36

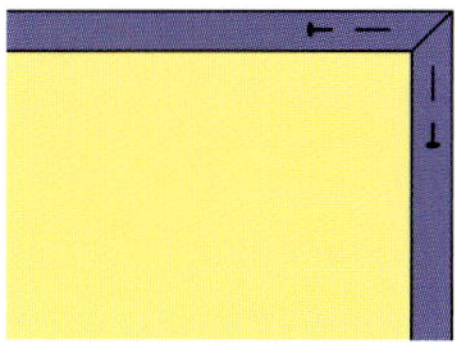

**16.** Blindstitch binding to backing, taking care not to stitch through to front of quilt.

## BLIND STITCH

Come up at 1, go down at 2, and come up at 3 *(Fig. 37)*. Length of stitches may be varied as desired.

Fig. 37

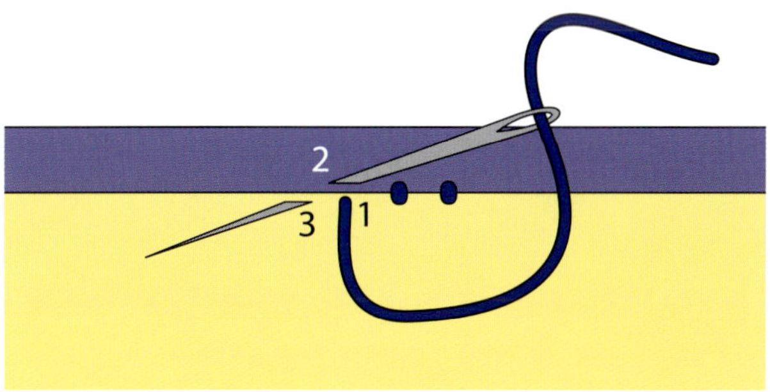


## SIGNING AND DATING YOUR QUILT

A completed quilt is a work of art and should be signed and dated. There are many different ways to do this and numerous books on the subject. The label should reflect the style of the quilt, the occasion or person for which it was made, and the quilter's own particular talents. Following are suggestions for recording the history of quilt or adding a sentiment for future generations.

- Embroider quilter's name, date, and any additional information on quilt top or backing. Matching floss, such as cream floss on white border, will leave a subtle record. Bright or contrasting floss will make the information stand out.

- Make label from muslin and use permanent marker to write information. Use different colored permanent markers to make label more decorative. Stitch label to back of quilt.

- Use photo-transfer paper to add image to white or cream fabric label. Stitch label to back of quilt.

- Piece an extra block from quilt top pattern to use as label. Add information with permanent fabric pen. Appliqué block to back of quilt.

- Write message on appliquéd design from quilt top. Attach appliqué to back of the quilt.

# Meet Nancy Rink

Passionate about fabrics of many styles, Nancy Rink is a quilter, designer, and dye artist who enjoys combining piecing and appliqué. "For me," she says, "nothing tops off a pieced quilt like a little bit of appliqué."

Admired for their exquisite stitching and color flow, her eclectic designs have won numerous national and international awards.

Nancy took the plunge as a full-time quilting professional after 23 years of teaching junior high and high school English. Nowadays, customers can shop for her fabric and kits and find her working at the Nancy Rink Designs studio in Bakersfield, California. As a licensed designer for Marcus Fabrics, she creates two to three fabric collections per year and the patterns to accompany them. She also develops block of the month programs for Marcus, some of which have included the popular Amish With a Twist programs.

Nancy has had quilts published in numerous quilting magazines and is the solo author of two earlier books published by Leisure Arts (*City Blocks #5735* and *Quilts to Warm Today's Home #5736*). She also has co-authored with her husband, Oliver, *Away From Home: Quilts Inspired by the Lowell Factory Girls* and *El Camino Real: Quilts Inspired by Early California History*.

For more information, shopping, and a gallery of some of Nancy's award winning quilts, visit her website, nancyrinkdesigns.com, and her Facebook page.

Production Team: Technical Editor – Lisa Lancaster; Associate Editors – Mary Sullivan Hutcheson and Jean Lewis; Editorial Writer - Susan Frantz Wiles; Senior Graphic Artist – Lora Puls; Lead Graphic Artist – Victoria Temple; Graphic Artist - Frances Huddleston; Photography Stylists – Angela Alexander and Lori Wenger; Photographer - Jason Masters